Broken for Good

A true story of betrayal, disillusionment and believing again

When you lose everything you thought would save you...

John Cox

"All Scripture quotations, unless otherwise indicated, are taken from THE HOLY BIBLE, NEW INTERNATIONAL VERSION®, NIV® Copyright © 1973, 1978, 1984, 2011 by Biblica, Inc.® Used by permission. All rights reserved worldwide.
Cover photograph: Cape Town, Chapman's Peak Drive. John Cox
Back Cover Photo: Jenny Geddes

Copyright © 2014 John Cox
All rights reserved.
ISBN: 0993875602
ISBN-13: 978-0993875601

Additional Books by John Cox:
Into Depression and Beyond (Kindle)
Googling God (2008) Published by Harvest House Publishers

Dedication and Acknowledgments

This book is dedicated to:

…My wife Sheryl, who has encouraged me to complete a very personal manuscript even though some of the recollections for both of us have been painful. Thank you for your patience, believing in the bigger picture, and your unconditional love and support. You are one very special lady and I love you.

…My adult daughters, Carmen and Michelle. This story very much involves you. I'm so grateful for your unwavering love through some difficult years and your willingness to forgive my failures and mistakes. I'm incredibly proud of you both and it's the joy and privilege of my life to be your father.

…To the community of Jericho Road Church in Port Alberni who has traveled with me on a long journey spanning thirty years. If ever there is a Christian witness to grace and generosity of spirit, it is surely found among you.

A huge thank you to my editor Mick Silva, who has challenged, encouraged, and coached me through the long writing process. I couldn't have written this story without your expertise, patience and perseverance to see it through to the end.

Most importantly, thank you God! I'd have nothing to say if it wasn't for you. This story is ultimately about your goodness, your power, and your desire to heal and restore. You're the hero, I'm the villain, and "Amazing Grace" is our song.

Though some names and details have been changed this story is true.

Contents

Dedication and Acknowledgments	iii
Author's Note	vii
Introduction	ix
The Kiss	1
Mother And Maids	5
Goodbye Dad	16
Betrayal	22
Losing Faith	36
Ivory Towers	44
Dead Man Walking	50
The Dark Side Of The Moon	58
Torn Apart	64
Trading Spaces	73
Man Of God	80
Double Standards	88
Breaking The Logjam	98
Exposing Superman	105
Hearing Again	111
Help My Unbelief	119
Persevering	125
An Unexpected Crisis	137
Jericho Road	141
Back To Africa	149
The Promised Land	157
Epilogue	167
A Short Interview	171
About the Author	175

Author's Note

Life can be an unanticipated disaster at times that yanks the rug from under your feet leaving you sprawling in the most undignified position. How does one describe their tortuous personal journey of moral failure, betrayal, disillusionment, despair and hope without implicating others or breaching confidences?

In the telling of my story I wish to respect the privacy and integrity of those involved. I've therefore chosen to only include details that align with that commitment. Many of my actions inflicted considerable pain and I do not wish to compound old wounds.

My purpose in writing is to encourage those who've known personal failure and struggled to experience restoration. For those who've tumbled into dark places and for whom lasting genuine hope has been elusive. For those disillusioned with Christianity and/or God and have walked away from ritual and religion.. For those who dare question and ask, "If God is so good then why…..?"

Some have given up on God and cannot imagine a future in the church as a place of safety or a source of exciting revelation. However despite all the flaws and many challenges I believe Christian communities can be redemptive wellsprings of healing and hope for people like me, who'd lost their way.

The telling of my story is a spiritual act of defiance and revenge against the one who seeks to steal and destroy. A refusal to allow failure and struggle to have the final word over my life; a declaration of hope.

God's the only one who can work such a miracle – his kingdom really does come on earth as in heaven. Here's one small example of how he's doing just that.

Introduction

In my teenage years I'd probably have written confused accounts about life's meaning and purpose; recounting tales of the youthful exploration of God, girls, surviving school, and a bewildered search for identity, vocation and purpose. It would no doubt have been idealistic and laced with anger at the unfairness in the real world. I had yet to appreciate the gift of grace.

In my twenties, my 'higher education years', I'd have written dissertations on life crammed with quotes from books, newspapers, and anecdotes from university. They, too, would pulsate with idealism and conviction about God's purposes for people, for cultures, for life and the whole wide world.

In my thirties I was settling into marriage, children, immigration to Canada, and career advancement. My focus would have been on God's faithfulness, provision and the relevance of his instruction for life. I'd have shared my belief in the hope and truth offered in relationship with Jesus. But if I was honest, I'd have confessed to some confusion about church denominations, theology, and the challenges of following Jesus. I felt a rising tension over my Anglican affiliation, which seemed akin to living with an angry arthritic parent. I sensed a growing need to identify and set boundaries.

By my forth decade I couldn't speak. The perfect storm broke. Disillusionment with institutional religion loomed large, my marriage cracked wide open, and a deep childhood longing threatened to drown me in self-pity and fear.

A long silence in darkness would last for more than eight years. I never dreamed the journey out would be so long and hard. I'd pick up books on depression merely to find out whether the author had survived and was still alive. "How did anyone make it through this hell?" I cried. As a pastor I had betrayed my calling. Judgment was swift. Unsolicited advice was plentiful. Comfort and caring friends were often hard to find.

I experienced depression and despair that took me to the very brink of suicide. My anger erupted against God, the church, professing Christians, business partners, corruption, and literally anyone who dared not see or validate me. I'd scrawl poems of unprintable fury, callous cynicism, self-pity, and bewilderment, desperate for help.

God's love was cruelly distant and lasting transformation (rather than the Band-Aid compromise I was more than willing to settle for) was not even a possibility for me.

The relief I begged for from Him finally came, but it bore no resemblance to what I thought I'd asked for. In a thousand years I would never have dreamed, imagined, or believed what would become of me, even less what I was capable of, and least of all how far He was willing to stretch to finally take hold of me.

This is my story of how I was broken for good.

By this time a lot of men and women of doubtful reputation were hanging around Jesus, listening intently. The Pharisees and religious scholars were not pleased, not at all pleased. They growled, "He takes in sinners and eats meals with them, treating them like old friends." (Luke 15:1- The Message)

The Kiss

For I know my transgressions and my sin is always before me. Against you, you only, have I sinned And done what is evil in your sight
Psalm.51:3-4

I kissed her in a hotel room while attending a Christian leadership conference. I'd asked my wife Karin to attend - wanting her to be there to protect or perhaps inhibit me, while secretly preferring that she stay at home so that I wouldn't be restricted. She couldn't come for a reason I cannot recall, even though she'd expressed concern about a simmering relationship that I insisted was nothing more than a friendship.

It was an evangelical Christian Conference I was required to attend for credentialing purposes as a pastor. Fifteen years earlier (1981) I'd been ordained as an Anglican priest. During the previous year, the congregation I'd pastored for twelve years left the denomination and became an independent church. I'd never met most of the people attending the conference and was basically jumping through hoops.

Catherine and her husband had been friends of ours for some years. She was a close friend of Karin's and they'd joined us for a couple of holidays with our respective children, who were of similar age and got on well together. Initially I'd shrugged my shoulders at the friendship, "Not really my type," I declared and did nothing to foster the relationship.

The years rolled by and circumstances in and around our church changed; conversations with Catherine increased. Little by little I discovered a kindred spirit and it tugged within, awakening parts of me I hardly knew. At first it was lingering conversations in the parking lot, then meeting for walks and talks that spilled into discussions about marriage and unmet longings. Intellectually I knew I was playing with fire but I never believed I'd lose control. I was quite familiar with Christian moral values and would have wholeheartedly agreed with fidelity in marriage, faithfulness to one's spouse, and integrity in leadership.

If the truth be known, my head, intellect, and rational thinking had received enormous input, attention and gratification over the past twenty years. In fact I'd believed that by pursuing education and prestigious degrees, my longing for being valued and recognized would be met. My marriage to someone with a respected medical career would complete my sense of security and fulfillment. All of this was good but I failed to understand that it was my heart that was hurting and malnourished. Mere knowledge and prestige were as sawdust to the hunger within - which I'd learned to live with to such a degree I thought it was just the way things were.

I remember holding a piece of wood quite close to the blade of a chop saw and thinking I'd be quick enough to pull away. I cut the wood and it kicked back snapping my fingers to within millimeters of the blade. I never underestimated the danger of that machine again; but in matters of the heart, I didn't escape unscathed despite my initial self-talk. I was like the addict in denial declaring to every concerned challenger, "I can stop whenever I want to."

Such was the road leading to the conference when the blade kicked back and this time drew blood; after a long time resisting I finally picked up and used. Catherine was my cocaine and I was hooked into the wildest and most terrifying ride of my life.

I'll never forget 'the kiss'. How the transgressing of the forbidden threshold released a passion that enveloped me - and it was no good thing. I knew the instant our lips touched. I couldn't help myself; here was someone who understood my innermost being. My deepest unspoken longings were attracted and pulled toward her, resistance melted – wax spilling from a dancing flame mesmerizing me. This was so much more real, tangible, and comforting than what I was getting from God or had experienced in my marriage for a long time. As with tasting the forbidden fruit in Eden - intoxicated by the deceptive promise of fulfillment and satisfaction, I was quite oblivious to the disaster ahead.

'The kiss' was utter insanity. Her husband was downstairs, their children at home. My wife and children were back in the same town, my position as pastor of a thriving church teeter-tottered in the balance. Nothing else mattered – enough – then. I'd cared genuinely and deeply for my family; I would've been contemptuous and harsh if I'd been on the outside looking in at my behavior. In this illicit embrace, my life, career, hopes and dreams became muddy and estranged, confused and incomprehensibly self-absorbed.

At last I felt intimately at home with another human being who understood and cared for me. I thought I'd stumbled upon a deep pool, an oasis in the midst of a barren escarpment. The words, rationalizations, feelings, situation, the mid-life dilemma; I never imagined they would be ascribed to me. The intensity gripped me with a power that felt energized from another source. Later I may have called it demonic, but at the time it rose up as authentic and what I'd always been looking for – the rush and thrill after plunging a needle into the bloodstream.

"This is wrong," Catherine whispered; we kissed again. She pulled away saying she had to leave….

Overcome by the moment, the perfume, and the contact I protested… "Don't go; you have the rest of your life to walk away."

Someone knocked on the door, and I opened it to find her husband smiling across the threshold asking if everything was ok. "Yes, come in," I replied, "I'm not feeling that great, we were talking about the speaker we've just heard." They left the room a few minutes later as we all pretended nothing was amiss. I thought to myself. "If that had been me knocking on the door I'd have been furious."

"How was the conference?" I was asked on returning home.

"Ok I guess," I responded non-communicatively. The deception burrowed into the marriage like hungry woodworms while on the surface the appearance of normal was a paper-thin veneer peeling at the edges.

Months passed, tensions rose.

"You have to end this meeting and talking with Catherine," my wife demanded.

"It's just a friendship, she understands me. It's fine for you, you have supportive family, I don't have anyone!" I responded in frustration – feeling panic. I was drowning; yet unable to extricate myself from this emotional whirlpool. I didn't have the strength, couldn't find a lifeline, and God appeared to be asleep or indifferent. I was sinking fast.

"Nobody would put up with such behavior in a marriage," Karin said.

"What's this on your shirt - looks like make-up?" she asked in the kitchen as I returned home late one afternoon. I looked down at the faint smudge that stained the white shirt above my heart.

"It was only an embrace, nothing more," I protested. How was I to admit my struggle, when I was finding it impossible to pull away from someone who seemed to hear my heart's cry?

"Well I guess you have some choices to make."

Mother And Maids

Why, my soul, are you downcast?
Why so disturbed within me?
Psalm. 42:5

A few weeks later the phone rang, breaking the silence of the rather strained atmosphere that had politely settled around Karin and me. My brother's voice from the other side of the world responded to my tentative "Hello?"

"Hi John, Robin here; I'm afraid I haven't got great news about Dad. His prostate is flaring up."

"What does that mean?" I asked.

"The doctor says he could live for six months or less as his vital organs are slowly shutting down. I thought you'd like to know so you can decide what you want to do."

Robin, my brother, was calling from Cape Town where we'd been born and I'd lived for the first twenty five years of my life. I absorbed the unexpected news after hanging up. I knew what I'd do and why – which was the primary source of my sorrow.

It was the same reason I declined to celebrate my coming of age birthday (21 in South Africa) with my family over 21 years earlier. "I thought I'd dealt with this!" I'd scream as infuriation erupted.

I'd felt abandoned in some measure for years. My father was an accountant by profession, an analytical thinker who loved philosophy and debates with no conclusion or resolution. Abstraction, an appreciation for thoughts and words, pragmatism and a propensity for 'not getting too personal' were values he held dear. Disclosure about family matters was definitely out of bounds; "You don't air your dirty laundry in public," he asserted more than once.

When it came to understanding and expressing emotion he was clearly out of his comfort zone. The thought of making an appreciative speech of thanks on my 21st birthday to my father and stepmother for all they'd done for me was too much. I couldn't get the words out with enough sincerity. Now on the eve of my father's death I'd rather visit him while he was alive than sit at his funeral listening to people applaud his life. I knew what would be said and wasn't so cynical as to disagree with his good qualities – there were many. But our relationship never formed. Consequently news of his impending death meant that any possibility of that happening was slipping away forever. Maybe three weeks with him would enable a breakthrough of sorts as well as ease the chaotic confusion at home in Canada.

It was a long journey to Cape Town via London with too much time to think. The last flight I'd made to the southern tip of Africa was three years earlier with Karin and our two young daughters.

Now I was fleeing a marriage on life support to visit a father who was dying. He didn't know how to be a 'dad', and Karin and I were adrift in a sea of confusion and an ever-widening chasm of tired communication. How on earth had we arrived at this place of frustration and estrangement?

I buckled the safety belt, reclined in my seat, and paged through the airline magazine I'd pulled from the pocket in front of me. A stranger sat beside me; once again I sank into the anonymity of a transient who was far too comfortable alone. My default was to withdraw and watch the world from a hidden place where nothing was demanded of me. Others may share intimacy and freedom in relationship but I didn't know how to enter that place with abandon.

Traveling alone was a metaphor for my entire emotional life. However what had once been sustainable was now proving too weighty as cracks threatened to expose the awful truth both to me, my family and friends.

While my demeanor appeared to be that of a mature man inside a child squirmed and fidgeted. I found myself awkwardly regressing. The little boy who'd been well-mannered in the background for years now craved nurture and 'mothering' and resolutely refused to be silent. It was intense and led to quiet, hidden, painful sobbing that felt embarrassing and childish.

If truth sets one free, then I was confused about my truth. I felt guilty about wanting a depth of acceptance and love that had thus far been so elusive. "Everyone has challenges so be thankful for what you have and honor your marriage covenant," I scolded the child. Such self-talk had worked before but now it fell on deaf ears.

It could have been as nakedly simple as yearning for someone to pick me up, hold me and whisper, "I've got you now, you're safe, everything will be alright." Legitimate arms somewhere willing to embrace my awkward and terrifying panic – whether warranted or not. Please walk alongside me. I couldn't find it with family, friends, or church – and even had it been available, I'd probably have brushed the proffered help aside unwilling to receive.

I'd become a half-living contradiction; invariably sabotaging the very thing I wanted. I didn't know how to give or show love with any freedom one-on-one. I was awkward and clumsy in the presence of personal intimacy while eloquently appreciating the concept.

The only place I found validation (so it seemed to me) was in the embrace of the mother of another man's children (excruciatingly awkward to admit - even now).

My mother died when I was twelve. She entered hospital for a hysterectomy and never came home. I'd had a premonition that circumstances were going to change. Six months earlier I stood at the foot of my Aunt Pam's bed and said, "I think something's going to happen."

My mother's dark wavy hair tumbled down to her shoulders framing a pale complexion and large brown eyes. She always wore red lipstick and red nail polish and tended to be gentle and reserved. That's almost all I know of her.

One afternoon, perhaps ten months before her surgery, I entered the sitting room where she was having tea with a friend. She wore an orange cardigan and a charcoal skirt and when she answered my question she called me 'Darling'. I wasn't used to the term. I left the room clinging to that wisp of endearment, the unfamiliar feeling of attachment and nurture. The brief moment left an imprint that's never faded.

In South Africa in the 1950's and 60's, middle class 'white people' employed maids and nannies to look after their children. "Whites

Only" signs were still common everywhere; on benches, public buildings, movie theatres, and demarcating seating and viewing areas for all sporting events.

Lenie was a short Malay woman with long flowing black hair. She took us for daily walks, cooked our meals, and woke us up in the morning. I have more memories of her than of my mother. She was deeply involved in my life and yet always 'knew her place'. She was my confidant, my friend, my protector, my provider, my nurturer, my surrogate mother – but always a servant. When Lenie left after sharing our lives for nearly ten years, saying goodbye was devastating.

I recall playing cricket in the street with my brother. Our little black dog 'Dopie' loved chasing cars. Off he went in hot pursuit yapping and biting at the spinning rubber when somehow he miscalculated and got himself under the wheels. I watched from a distance in horror as he rolled under the car. He picked himself up and ran back to me. I thought he was okay but he dropped dead at my feet. I was stunned. I ran inside and breathlessly told my mother. She wiped a tear from her eyes and said, "John, it's alright to cry," as I stood stoically in the doorway.

I wanted to cry. Instead I turned and left the room to rejoin my brother playing cricket; Dopie's dead body lying on the sidewalk awaiting my father's return from work. "Boys don't cry," was the mantra of the post war years. Along with, "Children should be seen and not heard."

I'd become a small self-sufficient island hidden from view. I was nervous, insecure, and scared of life, afraid that my parents would die in an accident. I would lie awake waiting to hear the car turn the corner and the rattle of the chain on the heavy steel garage door as my father pulled it shut. Such anxiety manifested itself in a battle with asthma during those early years.

The attacks would come at night. I would rock myself to sleep with an arm bent behind my head and the other beneath my side. I'd no idea how it started but it was the one position that felt comforting – or self-nurturing. I remember the worst onslaught of asthma walking up and down the hallway heaving for breath. I thought I would die as I slowly suffocated and my father phoned the doctor. He arrived a short while later and administered an injection and a tablet that I immediately vomited against the wall. Slowly the injection took effect, the anxiety subsided, and I could breathe again. Fortunately, true to his word, I outgrew the asthma as I entered my teens.

The day everything changed, I was sick and the same doctor made a house call to see how I was doing. As he prepared to leave, my mother mentioned that my brother Robin had a swollen cheek, perhaps from a kick in rugby although he didn't recall such an incident. Doctor Charnock proceeded to examine him and a few days later rushed him to hospital for more tests. I wasn't aware at the time of the severity of what was unfolding.

Robin was diagnosed with cancer and given three months to live. Later the doctors offered to experiment with radical surgery giving no assurance of success as they'd never performed the procedure before. They removed his jawbone from the chin to below the ear and replaced it with a rib. The result was regarded as a miracle. The trauma of three operations over a number of years and consequence of living with a disfigurement is my brother's story to tell. His recovery was wonderful (my grandmother said it was an answer to prayer).

I couldn't comprehend the details or the pressure on my distraught parents at the time. All I knew was that Robin received attention and ice cream at meals, while my sister and I were left in the slipstream of his crisis to gather up the few remaining emotional crumbs.

He was regarded as a hero as he battled through his operations, the shattering scars that made people stare, and the relentless struggle to overcome such a visible challenge. He excelled in sport and eventually became head boy of the prestigious school we attended. He still shrugs in bewilderment at my very different recollections of our family, my father and our childhood.

Thirty years later my life was disintegrating. The world as I knew it was falling apart and I could no longer ignore the little boy tugging unremittingly at my gut. No-one sees the inner disfigurement of an orphan spirit and the crippled limp of a lonely child. There are no accolades for showing up day after solitary day trying to survive on the outside while inside the hidden incessant battle rages - lost, frightened, and misunderstood. It must be similar to those returning from war with every limb intact but memories and psyches invisibly shot to smithereens.

Tensions in the home before my mother's death grew intense as my parents dealt with my her condition and my brother's frightening diagnosis. I remember trying to sleep with mum slamming the bedroom door and shouting at my dad. They were drifting apart and my father's poignant entries in his diary hint at this reality. Every evening he'd record his thoughts in his journal at his roll-top desk beneath the gold-framed portrait of an 18th century man holding a large feathered writing quill. .

The week before my mother went into hospital I asked her if we could play cards. She was going out for the evening with my father. I remember her turning toward me at the hallway table. She smiled and said, "We'll play when I come out of hospital."

"But you won't be coming back," I whispered quietly to myself. We never played games anyway.

In early April 1965 my mother underwent her surgery and a few days after the operation the phone rang in the hallway just before breakfast on a day I'll never forget.

Later that morning I was called out of the classroom by the school principal. Mr. Van der Bijl was a towering man who could be imposing and quite frightening to a little boy. But that day his eyes were soft as he gently placed his huge hand on my shoulder, "Cox, your father's just called and he's going to fetch you and your brother at 12:30," he told me without revealing any more information.

I returned to my desk quietly. Mr. Charlton was the master teaching us for that lesson and asked, "What was that about Cox?" I rose to my feet and replied, "I think it's something to do with my mother sir, she's been quite sick." He grunted, the classroom shuffled, turned heads bowed back to desks. I sat down alone with my secret, knowing that she'd already died and waited for the morning to end.

At noon my brother and I stood outside the school…. "I think mom's died," I said. Robin didn't reply and looked in the other direction. My father's car rounded the corner. I opened the door and climbed into the front seat, "Mom's died, hasn't she?" I blurted out before he could say anything. His craggy sunburned face displayed little emotion other than a sadness in his eyes. "How did you know?"

We didn't know how to articulate it, but it was not difficult to read between the lines of the events that had unfolded so quickly earlier that day. "Your mother died peacefully this morning, there were complications," he said. "Oh....," was all I could say. My brother was quiet. Neither of us cried. "Maybe we should go to the beach this afternoon," my father continued, "Pamela (my mother's sister) is at the house, she's beginning to get on my nerves."

After a light lunch, we drove to the ocean to escape my aunt – and my dead mother.

I sat in the sand on the beach not far from the tidal pool where I'd first lifted my feet from the ground. "I can swim, I can swim!" I remember excitedly proclaiming as I 'doggy-paddled' in circles in the shallow water. The sun was warm. My father didn't say much. I traced patterns in the sand with my fingers as the salt water drained from my hair down my face until I could taste the sea.

I wanted to tell everyone that my mother had died.

I don't recall anyone touching me that day. I must have looked like any other kid with his dad on the beach. Who'd have guessed? Life didn't skip a beat - continuing as if she'd never existed. The sun shone, the sand baked hot, waves splashed over brown rocks cradling the tidal pools where we'd fished. Secretly I was relieved there wouldn't be more shouting and tension at home. It was surreal and sadly distant. And to this day a mother is more a concept for me than a reality.

Later in the day a friend's mother called. My father wrote in his journal…

'Shortly after arriving back, Mrs. Swanson phoned to express sympathy and to ask if the boys would like to go to Clanwilliam (a town about 400 miles outside Cape Town with a large lake popular for waterskiing) for the weekend. They were keen and I felt it would be good for them to get away so off they went early on Friday morning.'

When we returned the following Monday, my mother's funeral was over and we all returned to our daily routines as if nothing had happened.

My father left for work and we went to school. I rode a bicycle the couple of miles to school and timed my arrival for 7:40am so that I'd pass Jennifer walking to the bus stop. She was the daughter of one of the schoolmasters and always smiled and said, "Hi John." My heart leaped at the sound of her voice and my name on her lips.

School was about discipline, surnames and maintaining a stiff upper lip. For a boy who yearned for nurture it was hard to find there what I didn't even know I was looking for. I loved Fridays and hated Sunday nights; school was to be endured.

But I could sing.

Music became the one avenue of expression and affirmation where I exceled. I played the lead role in a small opera about a chimney sweep, sang in the choir, and eventually was treble soloist in the school's prestigious choir. I participated for about six years. In this one place I felt I belonged. I unknowingly detected the faintest breath of God amidst the stiff formality, but he appeared to be like my father or a schoolmaster; not someone easy to get close to.

Home was managed by the maids after my mother died. They were there when I left for school and when I returned in the afternoon. Lizzie had come to work for us when my grandmother sold her large home and moved in a few years earlier. She had been with her for years and was the cook. Lizzie was a large lady who waddled around the house singing under her breath, grey hair wriggling from beneath her cap to feather an aging cherubic face. I spent many an afternoon at the kitchen table while she peeled the potatoes, shelled peas and prepared the evening meal. Sometimes we'd sit in her tiny room with boxes and cases piled high above the cupboard and the pungent smell of Vicks in the air.

Mary was with us for perhaps 18 months. She was about nineteen, certainly not older than twenty-one, and mischievous and playful with me. I must have been twelve years old at the time when the mysterious world of women and sex appeared over my horizon. Until then the only 'information' I had was the sight of my mother naked beneath a full length negligée. Another 'moment of research' was my brother and I 'needing to go' to the washroom while my father was shaving and my mother was in the bathtub. We rushed in and out snickering, "Did you see that?"

I'd come home from school and immediately make my way to the kitchen which was undoubtedly the warmest emotional space for me in the house. Mary would laugh and tease and my curiosity would pique when she undid the top button of her uniform and beckoned me to come closer.

One afternoon she was taking a bath and I climbed up to stand on the window sill and spy on her in the tub. She protested mildly then stood up. I watched the white suds slip down her glistening ebony skin with awestruck wonder as she giggled. I waited for her outside the washroom door and tugged at her towel. We went into her room and lay on her bed and I felt her breasts. I smelled the fragrance of her powder and when she encouraged me to remove my shirt I ran away scared by what I couldn't understand was happening to me.

It must have been a year after my mother's death when some longtime family friends matched up my father with Noelle.

Noelle worked in her father's business as the lead designer of children's clothes. She'd been married to a lawyer who was a colorful character in Cape Town, active in the vitriolic world of politics where he supported the outlawed Africa National Congress (ANC). He was in many ways an irresponsible boy who loved life, women, and booze. After their twelve year old son Tom was tragically killed crossing the road near their home the marriage disintegrated. When my father appeared offering stability Noelle soon became our new mother. We were enthusiastic.

They were married in a small Congregational Church one Saturday afternoon. A friendly Scottish Reverend Dunstan billowing smoke from his ever-present pipe (when not inside the church) talked to us children tucked in the front pew about being crew members on a ship embarking on a new adventure. My spirits rose at the crack in the door. Perhaps life was going to be alright after all.

Noelle and Lesley, her daughter, moved in with my father, his three children and my grandmother. Initially we settled in harmoniously. Noelle kissed us goodnight – which was novel – and my father appeared to be happy. A page was turned, a new chapter begun, my mother laid to rest and seemingly easily forgotten, and from the outside it was a match made in heaven to heal two broken families.

Within six months Noelle was emerging as something of a control freak and my father receded into the background while she ran the house. My sister, Gill had picked up the slack after my mother's death and at fifteen had taken upon herself the task of organizing family meals and 'being responsible'. Noelle's appearance meant she was brushed aside and before long she was either ensconced in her room or out with friends.

Meanwhile Robin was undergoing another surgery. It appeared that he was out of danger but still had chemotherapy treatments and disfigurement to endure. My father was very attentive to him and they bonded in a relationship that endured until dad's death. My stepsister was doted on by her mother, who having lost one child, was always fussing over 'Les'. She would be the sweetest star of photo-shoots modeling Noelle's clothes and appearing in the marketing campaigns for the company. New clothes were always hers to wear; 'Noelle and Les' became an inseparable duo while my father and Robin linked arms. Attempts were made from time to time to draw me in but they invariably backfired. I'd grown resentful of the obvious favoritism, Noelle's over indulgence and my father's lack thereof.

For a while Lesley and I were taken for riding lessons every Saturday morning. I was secretly terrified and dreaded getting on the horse each week, but I never told anyone. A normal fear, to be sure, something a little encouragement and empathy would have dissolved. But no one knew. When our lessons were completed, it was decided that Lesley would have another set and thus the pattern began; sibling jealousy fed the worm that grew fatter as it feasted in my heart.

One night, Peter and Nan, the couple who'd introduced my father to Noelle came over for dinner. That evening Peter played the guitar and we had a sing-a-long. I was enthralled and never forgot the ditty he sang.

From then on, I longed to play the guitar and was thrilled to receive one for my birthday. Yet within the year Lesley had been given an expensive guitar and lessons from her father, and I felt the resentment and anger build within. I think Lesley felt slightly embarrassed but there wasn't much she could do. It became one more example of the constant disparities between me and the rest of the world. No mother who doted and a father who'd emotionally departed and didn't know how to be present for all his children equally.

By the time I was fifteen my father became a passive critic and disciplinarian perpetually disappointed in me and berating my rudeness. My older sister had left home; my brother was the compliant and courageous cancer survivor, and my stepsister was favored by an overprotective mother.

This is the time in my life when I recall yearning for a real mother.

The year after mother died, Gill suggested we attend an early morning communion service to remember her. My father asked why we were up so early and left us to go about our business as best we could. We walked down the road in our school uniforms to join the Anglican priest and one other person in a quiet service in the side chapel. He was a kind older man, Reverend Hampson, with bespectacled twinkling eyes and a gentle voice. He welcomed us and said a prayer of thanks for my mother with as much empathy as he could offer. I still remember the dignified formality of the Anglican Prayer Book with the appropriate written petition to the Almighty. It was as cold and distant as my father when what we needed was someone to hold us tight so that we could feel the love of God through a person. Instead we ended with 'amen' and shook hands as we went off to school.

At dinner we answered my father's only question. "How was the service?"

"Fine thanks."

What might my mother and I have shared? Were some of her struggles rooted in not feeling heard or seen by her parents or the man she married? Some said we were very similar. I've shed tears for her since, but all the way through my 20's and 30's no one filled the strange void in my soul that only a mother can occupy.

Goodbye Dad

I am a foreigner to my own family, a stranger to my own mother's children
Psalm. 69:8

The plane banked above the sprawling Cape Flats and my heart leaped at the sight of Table Mountain and Devil's Peak growing larger beyond the wing tip. Cape Town was still home.

I found my father in relatively good spirits, whiling away his days reading, sleeping, or sitting in the sun on the back porch. He was a very private man. Having spent his entire childhood in boarding school he'd little personal experience of warm family life. His father was an austere Anglican Priest always appearing in public in uniform – black shirt, white dog-collar, and a crumpled cream jacket.

As was the case with many men of his generation who'd been to war, my father found solace in work, sport, gin and tonic, a weekly men's bridge foursome, and a stiff upper lip. He laughed and joked with friends in a jocular superficial manner. At dinner he'd refill his white wine from a large bottle retrieved from the fridge and placed beside his chair. Two glasses was his limit, the second preceded with liturgical predictability.

"More wine Noelle?" he'd ask.

"Yes please, just a little."

The liquid gurgled, "That's enough Brian…stop! You always pour too much," she'd protest with outstretched hand.

"Don't be silly, it won't hurt you," he'd reply replenishing his glass.

I took the opportunity to visit familiar haunts in Cape Town; my favorite being walking the long miles of beach near Muizenberg and Sunrise. As a young boy I spent many days during the summer holidays along these shores. I learned to body surf, ran along the hard brown sand at low tide, and helped local fishermen haul in dripping fishing nets. I loved the sound of the waves crashing on the shore, the smell of the salt and wind, and the wildness of the shoreline. This was one constant in my life – an unchanging familiar place. I walked above the high-tide line and remembered my first girlfriend Jackie.

This was the beach where we lay in the hot sun behind a sand dune kissing. It was intoxicating and alive. I felt loved and thought that maybe she was who I'd spend my life with! I sensed that Jackie wanted to settle down but I was unable to commit. I wasn't ready.

The last three weeks with my father slipped by. Despite all I wanted to say or hear little of any substance was shared between us. Day after day passed and he didn't venture out much. I took off each day to walk the beach or see old sights and then return home. In the afternoons I'd frequently find him dozing in a chair on the porch in the sun. I'd sit and talk with him after lunch about people we'd known. But I couldn't access his heart, except once…

"Do you have any regrets dad?" I asked.

"I never reached my potential. My life seems such a waste of time…."

He and Noelle had visited us for a week in Canada a few years earlier and attended a service I spoke at. My father's response was typical detachment….

"Not really my cup of tea but your people obviously like it."

I'd become used to longing for my dad to make me the object of his attention and affection rather than fitting me in on the way somewhere else.

The morning I was scheduled to leave for Canada we ate breakfast at the round table that had hosted every family gathering for as long as I could remember. I think it belonged to my mother, or at least she inherited it. Breakfast was cereal, toast and coffee. My father tore the toast into four pieces and placed them at the side of his plate. One piece was picked up - butter and marmalade splashed on with a knife wiped off on both sides, enough for one mouthful, and then the ritual was repeated.

I have little recollection of our conversation; there was no reference to his fast approaching end or final words of wisdom, advice, or anything like that; probably just comments about the weather or the grandchildren.

"Time to go," I said rising from the table.

Enough's enough, I thought as I packed my bags and took a last lingering look at the neat shelves of books in his library, his roller top desk, and the cerebral world that had been so hard to break into.

We walked in awkward silence down the narrow passage to the front door. Outside on the doorstep we shook hands...

"Glad to see you my boy, good luck."

"Thanks dad, goodbye."

I turned and carried my bags to the car. He stood at the door and waved, so much left unsaid between us.

Five years later my father's journals, a pile of black exercise books and diaries, were delivered to my house on Vancouver Island with a note attached from my brother, "I think these should be destroyed." I always imagined the day when I'd sit and read what my father wrote after he'd died and we could no longer speak face to face; a safe revelation for him, a little too late for me. Sorting through the bundle I found the one dated 1965 and opened it

Over thirty five years ago I'd sneaked into my father's bedroom one evening while he was out and borrowed his journal from his sock drawer. I was twelve and I wanted to know what he thought and felt when my mother died. Scared of being caught I'd quickly scanned the neatly written lines describing how my brother and I responded to the news of her death...

'At 12:30 as arranged with Mr. Van der Bijl I picked up John and Robin at the back entrance to Bishops and told them of Yvonne's death. They said they knew and expected it and received the news with extraordinary equanimity. This reaction by the children surprised me more than anything else.'

Extraordinary equanimity more accurately described young children who'd already learned how to 'not need nurture' and remain hidden.

All these years later on Vancouver island I could still feel the emotions rise within as I read of a young boy's isolation and stoic fortitude in the face of his mother's death. I sat by the wood fire in a favorite old rocking chair scratched to shreds by my two cats, the diary cradled on my lap; the moment I'd long imagined had finally come. I was an orphan. I wasn't angry with my father, just sad that the window into his heart was a posthumous glimpse through his writings.

"I don't know what your problem is with dad," my brother would say. "You're always blaming him for your life. I had a great relationship with him. You just didn't make the effort."

Our conversations on the matter invariably end in frustrated silence; as is the case with many siblings our experiences are different. I loved my father, he was a man's man, good at sport, a great dancer, a thoughtful man who read lots of books, and felt far more than he showed. I wanted to connect with his heart and couldn't find it except when as a little boy I'd stand on the bed and play barber and comb his hair. He'd tell us stories about Captain Cook that would be a little scary and our weekly summer trips to the beach were often accompanied by little songs he sang with us.

As we grew older the bond seemed to slip away as unknowingly I began to pull at his heart for more than he knew how to give. I'm sure it was because of his austere childhood in private boarding schools with no sense of family, the war years in the navy, an unhappy marriage, and the stress of trying to cope with three children who'd lost their mother. He was an accountant, a few years younger than I was now when his world was turned inside out.

I read of my father receiving a telegram that his father had died unexpectedly. I could have written almost the same lines: *'I had never known him very well. We had never done things as a family and he had never taken me out on outings or anything like that.... Ours was a strange relationship which grew stranger as we grew older.'*

The only other entries in my father's journal that year are entitled 'Yvonne' – my mother. They describe her preparing for her surgery.

'Yvonne was very quiet when we arrived back home and also on Monday morning. We said very little to one another and I was no great help to her when she needed sympathy and understanding. We had grown too far apart for that - years before.

When I went into the bedroom at 4:30 Yvonne was sitting on a chair by the window with her case in front of her. She looked like a frightened young school girl about to go to boarding school. I felt immensely sorry for her but at the same time helpless to give her the courage she needed...'

The next day she had the operation and initially seemed to be recovering well. The following day my father visited her in the evening after dinner....

I opened the door and went into her room. The light was off but there was a full moon and the moonlight streamed in through the uncurtained window....

.....We talked sporadically but mostly sat in silence. Eventually I took my leave. At the door of the room I turned and said goodbye. Yvonne lay with her face turned towards the window again and her eyes looking upward towards the night. The room was light in the moonlight. She did not answer and with a last look at her I opened the door and went out into the night light of the corridor. I did not see Yvonne again.

I rested the journal on my lap, flickering memories and emotions rising with the flames in the woodstove. I recalled the events that unfolded the next day as if it were yesterday.

It was early Thursday morning when the phone rang; a jangling alarm vibrating through the house. My father took the call; he was getting ready for work, white shirt, grey suit and tie. It was a hurried conversation at the black rotary telephone hanging in the hallway. Grabbing his coat he rushed out of the house, "I'll see you later, be sure to get to school."

"I'm not going to school," Gill announced to Robin and me as we headed out, "I'll wait for dad."

My father hung around the hospital having been warned that my mother's future looked bleak....

'I paced up and down on the front steps. It was a glorious morning. The sun was shining brightly. I tried to will Yvonne to live and made all sorts of resolutions to myself to try to be more understanding and sympathetic in future. For twenty minutes I paced up and down on that front step – up and down.'

Later my father returned home where my sister Gill (15 years old) was waiting......

'I noticed Gill's case was in the hall. I looked into her room and saw her sitting at her desk. When I asked her why she was not at school she said she was waiting for me to get back from the hospital. Rather bluntly I said, "I am afraid I have bad news for you. Your mother is dead." Gill did not react at all and after a minute or two I walked out of her room....'

On the next page he writes a comment about Gill's response - totally failing to comprehend the impact of his demeanor as a father sharing one of the most devastating moments in a child's life....

'Her (Gill's) reaction to Yvonne's death amazed me. At no time then or subsequently did I see her show any emotion. It was quite frightening...'

Sometimes doing nothing at all is the action that scars the deepest in the heart's hidden places. A father at the doorway and a teenage girl grieving the loss of her mother without tears, embrace, or tender words? My father could never cross the threshold into our rooms long enough for hurts to be noticed and do what only fathers can. Enter in, hold a hand, provide a shoulder to lean into, and promise to stay close until the light breaks through these darkest of times. Show you how to feel and cry in the presence of another in safety.

I closed the journal feeling surprisingly tender toward him. Speaking to the empty couch as if he were alive I said, "No-one crossed your threshold either, did they Dad? You passed the hole in your heart to me without even knowing it was there. We could've enjoyed so much more together ......"

Perhaps that's why years later as a pastor I wanted to be there for people and not abandon them to isolation when life went horribly wrong. My dilemma was that it was easier to do so for others than within my immediate family. Like my father I didn't know how to give intimacy; it was far too awkward an intrusion. Even when offered I'd instinctively withdraw despite the inner craving for that very thing.

But at least I was growing in awareness, so that when my friend Bill experienced a crisis I couldn't just let him sit there.

Betrayal

When my heart was grieved and my spirit embittered,
I was senseless and ignorant, I was a brute beast before you.
Psalm 73:21-22

"You're wasting your time, John. Don't get me wrong - I appreciate your visit but…"

I sat knee to knee with Bill in a weather-beaten wooden cabin out at Maclean's Mill, an historic sawmill tucked under tall cedars and maples near Port Alberni on Vancouver Island where our church was located. The railway from town stopped there. Every summer a carefully restored steam engine would haul carriages full of tourists to and from the Harbor Quay. Bill helped rebuild the smoke-billowing iron beast and oversee the restoration of the mill.

Now he was camping out there alone, marriage seized up and off the rails. We'd known each other for about ten years – since I'd arrived in Port Alberni as pastor of the church he attended with his family.

Darkness shrouded the room. Bill was silent, his grey head bent; the normal easy banter replaced by a furrowed brow. I'd enjoyed meals at his family table surrounded by teenage children in a casual and informal household. Over the years it wasn't hard to discern tensions between him and his wife. He often called her 'the dragon', usually amidst guffaws and laughter. I knew she was a challenge at times but all seemed stable as long as the medication was monitored. News of his departure was a shock and I'd promised to go out and have a chat.

"What's going on, Bill?"

Silence.

"How long do you think you'll be here? Is there anything I can do?" I asked leaning in. "You know how much you're loved and that God cares for you…." My voice trailed off in a whisper as the words fell from my lips, weak and wet, rather than strong with faith and power. It was painful to see my friend in such isolation. He'd spent hours helping me rebuild a Triumph Spitfire and was a wizard with engines, always willing to help. I knew that he wasn't fulfilled at home but you figure people learn to live with their situation, or at least try to initiate change. Sometimes the relationship gets neglected like the old Spitfire and when you eventually sit in the driver's seat and consider the investment it would take to fire it up the challenge is overwhelming.

"John I know you mean well but I'm done, I just can't do it anymore," Bill whispered.

"Is there someone else?" I asked, tears welling in my eyes.

"Yes, I met her during a business conference, she lives down island. Getting to know her merely confirmed for me what I've been diminished to and what our marriage has become." Bill stroked his greying beard and the wrinkled eyes that usually smiled were solemn pools of sadness. "I'm sorry John, I know it's not what you want to hear but it's over."

Our stilted conversation lasted a while longer before we shared an embrace and I stepped out into the rainy night. The brokenness and family fall-out would be devastating, and I'd be losing a friend. I talked to the steering wheel all the way home. "God I wish you were easier to get a hold of. Sometimes it seems you're so indifferent. It's hard to know what to say to guys like Bill. There's no way I'd ever get divorced or betray my marriage," I reassured myself with conviction and passion.

It was only when I experienced my own crisis of marital breakdown that I appreciated the place Bill found himself that evening alone on the outskirts of town. I wanted to shake him as others would want to shake me so that I'd come to my senses.

Friends hurt for each other and long to make things right but don't know how. It's so challenging to witness emotional pain in someone else when common sense bounces off them as they stagger toward what others clearly see as disaster.

I met Karin at university in Cape Town at a Christian house party over a weekend at Betty's Bay, a popular beach community outside Cape Town. I was attracted to her independence, strength of character, sharp intellect, athleticism and the fact that she was not 'obviously needy'. Meaning that she didn't demand any emotional support from me fraught with complexity arising from childhood abuse or trauma. If anything she offered me stability and a foundation of family I'd never known. Karin was a committed Christian, shared a vision for ministry and was totally supportive of the direction I was taking.

We dated for about fourteen months before I left for three years of theological study in England. We didn't maintain our relationship through that time because I was reluctant to be 'tied down'. She continued with her studies and took a year off to work full-time with a Christian organization in schools around South Africa.

Three years later, not long after returning to Cape Town, I nervously dialed her number.

"Hi, it's been a long time," I said.

"Welcome home, I heard you were back," Karin replied.

"I wondered whether you'd like to get together and catch up," I asked a little tentatively.

"Sure, that would be nice."

The following evening I picked her up from her student digs (shared house) and we drove around the front of Table Mountain, through Cape Town and shared a meal overlooking Table Bay. After dinner we strolled hand in hand along the illuminated walkway at Sea Point with salt in the air and the gentle rhythm of waves rolling lazily over the black rocks below. It seemed my homecoming was complete. Six months later we were married, assured that God had blessed us and that our marriage was aligned with his love and will for our lives.

My struggles years later had some roots here in the beginnings when it seemed that God's hand had been on my relationship with Karin from the start. To explain what I mean I have to shuffle back a year and introduce you to Anne. She was a lovely radiographer who decided after six months that our relationship wasn't going to work. I was heartbroken and for the first time in my life was open and vulnerable with my friends about how I felt. Normally I'd attempt to mask my true feelings. I could laugh and joke but expressing tenderness and vulnerability and admitting a need was unheard of. I thought to do so would make me weak and I preferred to be in control.

I lay on my bed and poured my heart out to God asking why everything had to be such a struggle? I told him that I was tired of these crashes and rejection, and there was nothing at home other than a place to sleep and eat. That's when unexpected thoughts infiltrated my mind - as if God were actually conversing with me.

He said, "John, you really love Anne don't you?"

"Yes," I replied, "You already know that."

"How would you respond to her if she asked you for something that you knew would be wrong for her, but in the moment of asking she couldn't see it?"

"It would be tough," I responded, "But I'd still say no."

"John, feel your heart for her now and understand that's how I see you; understand that I'm not enjoying saying no to you right now."

It took some time for this revelation to sink in but I remember the sting subsiding as I spluttered, "Ok Lord, but could the next person I'm involved with be the one I marry please? I'm longing for stability and a place to belong."

Some months later that person was playing the guitar when I walked into the house party and her name was Karin.

When we were married she still had a year to complete her medical training. My first appointment was a rather traditional Anglican Church in the middle class suburb of Claremont on the outskirts of Cape Town. We lived in a small apartment near the church and were excited to have our own home. I struggled with the formality of the church as my approach was more relaxed and contemporary. However I trusted that I was submitting to the process even though I felt manipulated by the institution. The Church placed priests in congregations dismissing character, personality, style, and gifting as of secondary importance. It was a religious model that depersonalized ministry and had a disastrous impact on many congregations because of the lack of continuity in vision and even teaching.

My frustration simmered and I found some measure of relief by enrolling to complete a Bachelor of Divinity (Hons) degree through London University. I still believed that credentials would mean something and help build integrity as I sought to balance passion and conviction with thoughtful teaching. Karin completed her degree and began work in a major hospital while being keenly involved with music and ministry when she could. We never had any disagreement about pursuing joint careers and were mutually very supportive of one another.

After two years at St. Savior's we moved to a large Black church called St. Cyprian's in Retreat. This was a vibrant congregation of about six hundred who had witnessed God's healing hand on a priest and many in their leadership who'd struggled with alcoholism. They shared dramatic testimonies of transformation and the church had blossomed over the previous ten years. It was a mix of robes, incense and enthusiastic singing, clapping and worship of Jesus.

Again I reluctantly submitted to the liturgical formality. I perceived the rituals as creating distance between God and ordinary people that merely elevated the status of clergy unnecessarily – an 'us and them' mentality. However the passion and obvious faith of the people was genuine against the backdrop of political unrest and police brutality that was increasing across the country.

Considering a future for the children we didn't yet have we explored emigrating; South Africa was a volatile and uncertain place to live and the future very unclear. I was attending a conference when we received a phone call from Vancouver Island asking whether I'd be interested in a leadership position with an Anglican church in Port Alberni. I'd never heard of the town but I knew in my spirit as soon as the call came through that we'd be going there.

One of the guest speakers was the principal of Regent College in Vancouver.

"What's it like on Vancouver Island?" I asked

"Vancouver Island's beautiful," he answered in his Canadian accent. He looked distinguished with neatly trimmed grey hair, of average height, sporting conservative grey pants and chequered shirt complete with tartan tie and a cashmere sweater. "I'm not sure about Port Alberni though; it's a logging town beginning to experience some hard times as the industry changes. It's probably great; I've never actually been there," he replied with a smile.

"Well it has to be better than living in this powder keg of uncertainty," I thought to myself as I walked away with a sense of anticipation rising in my spirit.

After interviews and immigration formalities we finally arrived on the West Coast in the latter half of 1985. I was Senior Pastor of St. Alban's Anglican Church and Karin eventually shared a practice as a General Practitioner and worked three days a week.

In Port Alberni we lived in a beautiful Cape Cod style house owned by the church and after a year were both sensing with excitement that it was time to begin our family. And because we didn't own our home we began looking around for a place to call our own that might also offer a place of retreat for family holidays.

Situated amidst a cluster of islands between Vancouver Island and the mainland Saltspring provided the ideal getaway that was not too far away while being easily accessible

We managed to purchase our ideal property one day before our future neighbors visited the same site and would have snapped it up. Over the next years we holidayed there with our young children while I built small structures to enhance what was initially a camping site.

It was the first property we'd ever owned and helped me feel that at long last I belonged and had somewhere to call my own. The church was growing, two healthy daughters were born and for ten years we visited the island on weekends, days off, and holidays. I continued building a washroom, a tool shed, and a funky shelter where the creepers grew and the kids swung in the hammock.

At first we had a large tent, then a fourteen-foot trailer on the building site and finally a small cabin was trucked up the drive and left balancing on blocks. I dug foundations and gingerly lowered it onto the concrete posts.

A nearby lake was a community swimming spot where the girls spent hours jumping off the dock and learning to swim. I was living my dream with two dogs in the yard, campfires roasting marshmallows after long hard days of reading and swimming, maybe a game of tennis or golf and a walk downtown. I was at my most content building something….. refinishing the interior of the rustic cabin, fabricating a bay window above the kitchen sink, planting apple trees, or completing a deck anchored into the steep mountain slope to enhance our viewing area by the fire pit.

Despite all these 'answers to prayers' Karin and I somehow missed the essence of one another. It's hard to know when or how we slowly drifted apart or perhaps neglected each other; I don't fully understand the mystery of that erosion other than the threadbare excuses and explanations that are woven through my story. Perhaps it was a mixture of inattention and avoidance without more mature people to mentor or walk alongside us. I was definitely the 'distancer' controlling our relationship, confused by emotional intimacy. Later I'd question my behavior, relentlessly wondering what my problem was with freely inviting Karin into my heart or declaring that I needed her.

We could do things together but being present to hear one another on the inside with tenderness and respect was awkward. We each waited for the other to take the initiative and were better at butting heads than opening our hearts or taking risks to help one another. Maybe we were too quick to offer advice rather than listen empathically to the heart behind the words.

How can one give away what has never been deposited in the first place? I had little experience of a parent embracing me unconditionally with love and affirmation and in my instinctive fight for survival I didn't know how to dismantle the invisible fortress I no longer needed. It would take me years to discover that no human can answer the cry of an orphan heart or slake the thirst of a spirit reaching for a father's affirmation.

As a General Practitioner Karin enjoyed a career and professional life quite independent from mine. On reflection I think we managed very well as a dual career couple but as time went by the work and busyness wasn't satisfying either of us. She relished hiking and physical activities as expressions of love and 'doing things together'. I was more comfortable with a less rigorous lifestyle although we shared a passion for our children, sport, music, and our Christian faith.

Karin expressed bemusement that I could talk to hundreds of people with relative openness and transparency and yet with her I was awkward – which was true. Later during counseling we were told that's quite a common occurrence. "You feel safer in front of crowds because they don't need you in a close or dependent way where an immediate response is asked for or expected."

From my perspective Karin didn't understand me, or know how to reach me and it was unfair to weight her with such expectations. I wanted a lover and a mother who gave unconditionally without pressure to return the favor and share 'me' – whoever that was. Our respective 'unmet longings' silently grew like mold or cancer in the dark places we seldom acknowledge or visit.

The intensity of my inner craving for nurture and validation overwhelmed me; Catherine became my emotional mother, friend, confidant, and lover and filled a void that neither God, the church nor my marriage had accessed.

For a short while I believed I could sustain a legitimate friendship with Catherine while honoring my marriage - my emotional arteries were clogged. Talking to the brain while the heart is breaking is as futile as trying to quench a thirst by taking a bath. I was quite aware of what was the 'right thing' to do but something within me had been tapped that was proving far beyond my ability to contain.

I thought I'd dealt with my lost childhood and the embarrassing 'longing for nurture'. Comparatively, I'd enjoyed a privileged lifestyle that would be the envy of many.

Up until the affair, I'd always had a panacea; education, ministry, then marriage, then emigrating to Canada, then children, then building a vibrant church. All the while deep within me was an unresolved emotional fear of being trapped. My unrest was so deep, I could never commit and the back door of my heart remained perpetually unlatched. Karin was unwittingly drawn into a no-win relationship and I didn't know how to acknowledge the existence of that unlocked door or how to quiet my embarrassing confession. I prayed, went up for healing prayer at conferences asking God to touch even what I was unaware of, and learned to live with my emotional limp as best I could. I figured it was manageable and something I had to accept; not comprehending what was growing in the shadows.

I grappled for explanations. I'd given my heart and soul to the church but it felt as if the institution was cut from the same cloth as my father. The message I received was conform, don't challenge or question, and your input and perceptions are not welcome. I knew instinctively this was not the whole truth. Over the years I knocked on the windows of leaders and the doors of people I admired, desperately seeking relationship and friendship, but all I found was impersonal professionals. Maybe that was a description of how Karin felt when trying to engage with me, and like them I too was blinded by the planks distorting my vision.

All the understanding and justifications failed to keep a lid on the emotions that poured forth - wreaking havoc and destruction. As my inner despair grew, so too did the sense of utter futility and meaninglessness of my life. The monster within broke the surface like a breaching whale shocking my senses and shipwrecking my marriage, my family, my career, and any sense of self I'd ever known.

Karin and I would bump into brief conversations that tiptoed on the fringe of intimate revelation and I'd usually be the one to back off. She tried to understand me but I felt inadequate or somehow inferior. She always gave the impression of having a solid handle on life and seldom appeared weak. One weekend she returned from a conference focusing on personal growth and inner healing. "They told me that maybe I have some things to work on as a mother and wife," she confided. I remember sighing with relief, thinking but not saying, "Oh wonderful, it's not all entirely my fault then."

On another occasion in this struggle for mutual understanding her vulnerability burst forth in a despairing exclamation, "I don't find my identity in being a doctor, I get it from being your wife and how you relate to me, how you see me as a woman."

"What do you want me to do?" I stuttered awkwardly. It was amazing to me that I could converse in a counseling situation with others and appear to have all the answers, yet when my wife spoke face to face with me I wanted to run out of the house screaming in claustrophobic hysteria.

"You don't have to do anything, just see me sometimes, tell me you love me, complement me on how I look, desire me. Don't tell me you don't know how, you flirt with half the other women in the church and I notice...."

"Well maybe it's because I know I'm safe…. It won't go anywhere," I replied lamely - playing dumb while thinking, "Everything she wants I can give to Catherine quite uninhibitedly but here it's so hard."

By the time my father died (in the fourteenth year of our marriage) Karin and I were struggling but managed the growing elephant in the room with avoidance or denial. The eventual betrayal was never a cold-hearted decision or single move but rather a gradual seduction under the guise of legitimacy and friendship. I found someone who appeared to comprehend my inner turmoil and validate my emotional longings which were still awkward and embarrassing to me.

Meanwhile, Catherine and I talked and went for walks. I should have known better and followed the practices common in ministry: don't meet alone with someone of the opposite sex.

When Karin asked me (quite rightly) to end the friendship I protested that it would be fine, nothing was going to happen; "You have your family, I have no one," was my crazy rationale. The truth was the situation was spinning out of control as I began to imagine life with another person while minimizing the damage that would inevitably result. While my head was filled with confused thoughts my heart crept out to find another source of sustenance – come hell or high water.

Over the years it was not unusual for me to spend a few days at Saltspring on my own. Except this time I caught a ferry across to Vancouver and rendezvoused with Catherine. She'd become like a drug I couldn't do without and from my emotionally hemorrhaging perspective the only safe place in my increasingly fragile world.

Faith and trust in God had already slipped away. My years of attempting to stand up for Christian integrity in the Canadian Anglican Church had left me isolated and emotionally spent. I'd anticipated support from other clergy and instead it felt more like falling off a moving ship and watching it disappear over the horizon. Life went on and I was left on a remote island with deep conviction but not much else. Others depended upon me for sustenance while I was struggling to find a cup to drink from myself.

The Church had been a place where I'd hoped to find a community and some affirmation, perhaps a family with friends and mentors. Instead it was another deep well of dust and ashes. Lined with square-bricked officials devoid of vision, policies, strategies, countless committee agendas and meetings it had run dry of relational joy or spiritual substance from which to draw.

The ferry docked in Tsawwassen about twenty minutes from Vancouver City center. The metal walkway glistened wet as I walked hunching my shoulders against the rain. "Good to see you," I whispered in Catherine's ear as we embraced. "I nearly didn't come," she replied, "I feel as if I've a large red 'A' hanging around my neck."

We drove to my hotel in Vancouver. We didn't spend the night together although it was a close call. Our liaison was passionate, intense, and reckless and for those fleeting moments it stopped the bleeding and satiated our mutual thirst; except we were never alone. Guilt and fear stood watching and the shame of our betrayal was ever present. Neither of us could relax nor consummate this longing for validation and the elusive homecoming of our hearts.

"No one will ever understand," I angrily screamed inside. "This is a bloody cliché and I can't find the escape hatch. Why are those who feel so desperate and take action always the criminals, while the ones who don't appear as innocent victims? They garner sympathy and we receive rocks and wagging fingers. Desperate people don't hurt others for fun!" My thoughts yelled heavenward, "God, damn it, where have you been?"

The following evening Catherine drove me to the ferry terminal after we'd spent a day in Vancouver. As we embraced in the parking lot a car drove up and shone its lights directly into the front window and I wondered whether someone we knew had spotted us.

The whole episode was foolish and irresponsible but the emotional connection filled my void. Catherine was accessing a place in me that I didn't know existed and the intensity that arose between us was irresistible – from both sides.

I sailed on the ferry through the darkness back to Saltspring, my heart heavy as a gravestone. Leaning over the deck rail I watched the flickering lights of island homes drift by and I pondered my betrayal and secret with shame. Now I regretted making the trip and was afraid. I sensed the hand of God lift, I'd pushed the envelope too far and was desperately trying to regroup and make amends. Negotiating with God in pleading prayer, repenting, "Please give me one more chance to work things out with Karin". I was terrified of what lay ahead no matter which way it unfolded.

"This cannot continue I resolved, I've got to stop the craziness, it's not fair to anyone."

The next morning I called home but it was too late…..

"Have you heard from the church elders?" Karin's tone was troubled but resigned.

"No, why?" My heart pounded above a sense of growing panic.

"Peter, (Catherine's husband) found the poem you wrote her hidden behind the piano and called. He read it to me; how she's your oasis in a desert place and how much you love her," her voice cracked. "I contacted the elders and asked them to deal with you as I've given up. You'd better get back here."

I stumbled from the telephone booth, retrieved a few belongings from the cabin and began the long journey 'home'. This was worse than any deaths, army training, broken relationships, or family tension I'd faced before. I was shattered.

"I'm done," I thought as despair enveloped me. "Why didn't she talk to me first, I was resolving to stop, I know it's crazy. Everyone will fixate on the juicy surface drama and not comprehend my struggle at all. This is going to be the talk of the town."

Karin was understandably in tears and I was angry at her calling the leadership before talking to me. "I'm tired of asking you to stop," was her response. I was humiliated, angry at her taking control, and without a leg to stand on. The elders convened a meeting at Catherine's house with her husband present, she was not there. They would be talking with her later.

What does one say? The line I crossed was indefensible, a gross betrayal of trust and Christian values. I felt like Bill Clinton trying to explain that he didn't have sex with Monica Lewinsky; technically perhaps not, but no linguistic gymnastics could extricate me from the predicament.

It was the man inside the pastor who writhed. I might lose my job but how do I 'never see her again'? Without her I was emotionally destitute. But she was another man's wife for God's sake! I felt like a screaming kid grabbed and pulled away from his mother to be kidnapped to a far-off land. That deep primal longing so beyond articulation had been awakened in the boy who never cried. Like rain falling in the desert and a flower blooming from a dehydrated seed swelling in joyful response.... only to wither and die unable to sustain the bloom without moisture. Even so, this was an illegitimate awakening and an inappropriate blooming. Try telling my heart and spirit that!

There were so many 'truths and lies' spinning around inside me. The parent in me said "smarten up you're behaving like a spoiled brat."

The child just cried, and cried…. "It's no use, I'm trapped." I withdrew inside and hid. "Do whatever you want with me," I whispered.

How does one shape acceptable words around what you've never known how to articulate; or that the revelation of what was missing was given in the finding? It was the illegitimacy of it all that wrapped a noose around my neck, placed a hood over my head, and stabbed my heart.

The next day I offered my resignation as the gaping hole of blackness sucked me into a place I never knew. I was overwhelmed - without argument or legitimate defense. I'd compromised my integrity, was unquestionably guilty of moral failure, but hurt so deep I could barely function.

The church leadership was gracious even though stunned; I'd been with them for more than twelve years. Some of them had come to a living faith in God through my ministry; I'd counseled others, married and buried their relatives, our ties went deep. I'd betrayed their trust and had little to say other than to splutter 'I'm sorry'.

The leadership never mentioned resignation; instead I was offered counseling and four months sabbatical to get help. I accepted and rolled over on the couch; tangled up in anger, despair, unfairness, loneliness, misunderstanding, powerlessness, fear, confusion, and guilt. I'd nowhere to hide except inside me.

Karin couldn't comprehend that this was about much more than infidelity (and most people would empathize with her – including me). Infidelity loomed so large that it crowded out the possibility of seeing anything else; she was betrayed by her husband and her best friend. My sense of abandonment towered equally imposing in the center of my psyche; both 'edifices' separated us from finding common ground that was mutually helpful, affirming and validating.

Everyone and everything was slipping away – even God. I'd poured my life and heart out for him as much as I knew how….. why had he allowed this to happen? The complete lack of understanding of my deeper emotional need and the causes for the emotional affair brought an utter hopelessness and futility. I felt indescribably misunderstood by my family, the church, wife, and even God. All of the blame and responsibility for what had transpired slashed through my heart as fingers, real or imaginary, pointed accusingly at me from every direction.

The couch became my grave and I buried myself, rolling a stone across the entrance so that even when one or two approached they encountered the silence of a cemetery.

At long last the little boy on the beach with the taste of salt in his mouth after his mother's death had been hugged and held, only to be ripped away again. How could anyone know or possibly understand? And even if they did, my source of comfort could never be legitimized. I knew what was 'right' but had no ability to exercise faith to trust God. There was no way out.

Losing Faith

Save me, O God, for the waters have come up to my neck. I sink in the miry depths, where there is no foothold. I have come into the deep waters; the floods engulf me. I am worn out calling for help; my throat is parched. My eyes fail, looking for my God.
Psalm. 69:2-3

The four months granted me by the church leadership to get my act together stretched ahead as I lay on the couch facing the wall's blank stare that Christmas. In the bleak mid-winter God may as well have been a million miles away, his presence eroded from my heart forming another grand canyon. I'd attended countless conferences over the years and had always been willing to be prayed for - imploring him to touch my life. Why hadn't he helped me in these dark areas of longing? I interpreted his silence as indifference; yet another betrayal, in utter frustration I gave up on him too.

My personal circumstances tended to be my yardstick for determining how close I was to God and whether I was 'in his will' or not. Peace and success meant 'yes'; chaos and struggles made him harder to find. It was a confused and inaccurate barometer of our relationship, or lack thereof, and at this stage he seemed impotent and uncaring. I'd totally lost sight of objective truth – much like visiting the Grand Canyon in heavy fog and concluding that nothing was there because I couldn't see anything. Sixteen years earlier the weather was clear when I stood on the South Rim.

During my student years I spent three summer months in the United States and Canada; much of the time circumnavigating the continent utilizing a Greyhound student ticket. I'd slept in the overnight bus from San Francisco before it rolled into the parking lot at the Grand Canyon after a long day.

I shouldered my backpack and walked across to the lodge wondering where the Canyon was situated and then I saw 'it'. Exquisitely eroded rock formations drenched in umber yellows, browns, and purples dripped deep into the ancient cracks. One of those rare and unforgettable occasions when silence bursts with music; the heart soars and the spirit sings with delight, there is no hint of let down or anticlimax. The scene before my eyes was breathtakingly beautiful, the Grand Canyon at sunset.

Early the next morning I strolled along the South Rim as the rising sun illuminated entirely different angles and vistas of the sandstone rocks and cliffs. It wasn't the quiet stillness of the morning, nor the soft mist rising grey from the river below, nor even the birds and sounds of a waking dawn that filled my senses. It was the light that stole my breath away.

How different would it have been if I'd arrived at the Grand Canyon on a cold wet day when it was battered with rain and wind? Or when fog settled low over the mountains and sunk its thick grey fingers into the riverbed? I might have cast one glance, shrugged my shoulders and headed indoors to escape the elements. My impressions and memories would be entirely different, recollections undoubtedly focused on weather conditions rather than the Canyon.

In my early years God often seemed hidden in camouflage gear somewhere in the midst of 'church'. There were moments when I thought I'd found him (like a kid jumping on his dad screaming with delight, "Gotcha!"); then a joyful personal connection infiltrated my spirit despite the dusty books and the stiff prison bars of religion. I intuitively sensed there was more to God than prayer books and choir boys singing scripted responses every week, joyless formality and Lent. Those glimpses were fleeting but enough to create a hunger and a longing to know and experience more.

It could have been a feeling when singing in the choir every Sunday, or participating in a large annual choral concert (1964-67) performed in the Cape Town City Hall. An arm's length from my feet the man pounding kettle drums puffed clouds of smoke from his well stoked pipe. The huge choir sat behind the orchestra with anticipation swelling as instruments were tuned and the hall filled to capacity. How can one sing Handel's Messiah and climax with the Hallelujah Chorus without being moved in the depths of one's spirit?

But even that stirring failed to translate into love, or my comprehending that God possessed character and personality. I eventually tired of Chapel services and singing in the choir in a boys-only school although I enjoyed the sense of belonging and the recognition I received. God appeared to be interwoven as model of good behavior and a theme for musical excellence, rather than having much relevance to my life. I was a lonely insecure boy whose mother had died and whose family functioned more like a harbor where we docked for the night under the same roof. Much of 'me' lived hidden on the inside as I learned to survive with minimal support or input from those around me.

Desperate to escape my social isolation and awkward fear of girls I attended a youth group in a small Methodist church a few miles from home. My sister had broken the ice a few years earlier and seemed to enjoy it. As soon as I was old enough I nervously ventured into this unknown place where they talked about God and girls were present.

We played games amidst plenty of laughter and activities, duster hockey pounding a tightly bound pair of socks with rolled up newspapers. I timidly initiated hesitant conversations with a few girls – but I was woefully shy and quite out of my depth. Every Friday we'd fill the small hall and on many occasions the evening would end with a guest speaker. I was introduced to people who lived and talked as if God was alive today; he actually spoke into their lives and influenced their choices.

They read the Bible and said that if I did the same I too would hear God's voice. Best of all I learned about God's love through Jesus. I was always feeling insecure and guilty of something. The shell in which I had retreated began to crack at the prospect of someone out there actually loving me, caring for me, and in whom I could confide without fear of being dismissed.

Acceptance and friendship drew me closer to discover more of God in the midst of a group who welcomed me and gave me a place to share my life as a teenager desperately looking for such friendship and love. On the outside I was cool, quick-witted, used sarcasm as a defense, and relished the demeanor of a rebel.

My years at Mossop Hall youth group (1966 – 70) introduced me to a personal God through his son Jesus. Even though I knew he loved me I was still wary that he'd be a killjoy if I risked too much. One thing I was sure of - there had to be more to life than me. Through those years I was enticed, encouraged, and dared to pry open the door to another dimension –pushing open the back of the cupboard as in C. S. Lewis's Narnia epic to discover for myself what lay behind old coats of tradition and mothballs of religion.

I was most impressed by some of the people who addressed us on Friday evenings. They were men who were personable, successful, and who talked about Jesus as their friend. I'm thinking of Bert Phful a business man and father of a well-known provincial cricketer, and John Gibbon, the headmaster of a co-educational school who was always trendy and dynamic. These men inspired me with their confidence and the ordinary non-religious manner in which they shared their faith in Jesus. It was a novelty to me as all I'd been exposed to were professional clergy and a very impersonal Anglican liturgy.

Later at university it became cool to be Christian. 'Jesus People' were identified by long hair, sandals, guitars, peace, and a casual unashamed proclamation that Jesus was alive: a much more satisfying friend than marijuana. They gave me permission to be myself. Through them I witnessed Jesus of Nazareth walking among ordinary people without posture or hype and I was invited to converse without someone else's script.

I tentatively reached out to touch him and my spirit was awakened as a void began to be filled. This revelation of God was intimate and personal. I was drawn to their uninhibited passion expressing love and gratitude for Jesus. At the same time I was nervous and self-conscious at exuberant waving hands in worship and the informality of the meetings I attended.

That's when I finally declared my intent to follow Jesus wherever He wanted to lead me. Without much mentoring or guidance it was a journey of many turns, trials, and errors.

It was probably inevitable that the momentous decision to serve God began with a rather vague sense of direction that took me at least five years to clarify. In 1973 I dropped out of university half way through a degree, worked with an animal charity for two years, before finally returning to complete a BA degree majoring in Psychology. I'd thought perhaps I'd become a teacher psychologist and considered pursuing Honors in Psychology to that end. But the tug to follow Jesus into full time ministry was also strong; except the Anglican Church, which was all I knew, wasn't hugely attractive to me. I'd discovered Jesus in the marketplace and that's who I wanted to serve and emulate.

"Why don't you join the community at Bishopscourt with Bill Burnett?" my friend Simon suggested. "I know him and can arrange an interview with one of his chaplains."

Bill was the Archbishop of Cape Town (head of the Anglican Church in Southern Africa), a conservative social activist clergyman and bishop until God surprised him after lunch.

"I was sitting reading the Sunday paper around midday when I felt God prompting me to go to my chapel," he told me later. "That kind of thing didn't happen to me but I couldn't shrug it off or ignore it. Reluctantly I put down the paper and went to my chapel and when I was up at the front it felt as if I was being pushed down to the floor. A great power came over me and I started praying with a new vibrancy and language; it was like a deep refreshing well opened up inside me. My whole focus was turned to Jesus and I found myself worshipping him.

Now I was a respectable liturgical bishop at the time and this event turned my entire life and ministry upside down and inside out. I was no longer interested in boring church meetings and that kind of stuff, I just wanted to talk about Jesus you know..." and he smiled. "Then they made me Archbishop, how ridiculous is that!" Then he added, "But you know, many years ago when I was an escaped POW standing outside a cave in the hills in Italy God told me that one day I would be a leader in Cape Town. And here we are."

After a pleasant chat over coffee with the chaplain it was agreed that I'd live at Bishopscourt and work in the office for a very modest subsistence salary. It's one of the historic buildings in the southern suburbs of Cape Town, built in the seventeenth century as a sprawling two-story residence surrounded by gardens. It would be my home for nearly a year and during that time the course of my life changed dramatically.

I'd been part of the community for about six months when I blurted out over lunch, "It feels as if I'm receiving so much from living here without much opportunity to give it away."

It so happened that Bill and a team were about to travel to Durban to lead a week of teaching and 'renewal of faith' in a local church. The next morning he invited me to join them and help lead the opening worship (as I played the guitar and sang). I knew immediately that God was up to something; this trip was more about him working on me than anything I had to offer. Frankly I was nervous about talk of God empowering us with his Holy Spirit and working through us. I believed it as a concept, but Bill was taking it to another level – where he actually anticipated encounters with God would happen! I was used to people praying but not expecting anything to take place – it was much safer that way, and extremely predictable and boring.

On the first night of the teaching week Bill said that he'd talk for a while after the opening worship. When finished he would invite people to come to the front if they wanted prayer for God to work more powerfully in their lives. He then proceeded to include me among those who would pray with anyone who ventured forward. My heart sunk, I didn't want to do that – nothing ever happens when I pray. But I couldn't get out of it; after all he'd paid for my ticket to come along and I'd said I wanted to be stretched.

When the moment came for people to respond I was hoping they wouldn't. Of course my pleadings with God fell on deaf ears and many came forward thirsty for more. I felt sorry for the fellow who ended up with me, having to suffer through my stuttering awkward counsel and prayer. It seemed rather pathetic to me and I finished up that day feeling quite dejected.

The following evening the same thing happened. This time I was with a lady who felt that she was spiritually 'stuck'. For some reason I sensed that God wanted her to receive more of Him and His gifts; except I didn't pray for that kind of thing. I looked up as Bill happened to be walking down the aisle. Waving him over I explained that this lady would like prayer for God's power to work in her life in a new way. Bill smiled and invited me to be seated on the other side of her. He was a tall and very gentle man. He spoke with her for a while and removed any sense at all of anxiety or pressure.

Bill described God's great love for her and His faithfulness before suggesting that we pray and trust God to answer however He wanted to. She might receive a gift right then, or perhaps sometime in the future. What was vitally important was for her to relax, receive, and not to worry about the outcome. We prayed and nothing visible happened. Bill calmly and confidently thanked God that He'd responded to the cry of her heart, gave her a hug and went on his way quite assured that God would honor what we'd requested.

Meanwhile God spoke to me quite clearly and gently in my mind. "John, you thought that if you prayed for that woman nothing would happen, and if Bill prayed it would make the difference, didn't you?" "Well I guess so," I muttered. "What happens when someone is healed, who gets the glory?" "You do Lord no matter who prays," I said.

"John if that is true then what's the problem? Your task is to bring people to me and allow me to determine how I'll respond and what will happen. Stop worrying about the answers, just do your part – bring people to me and don't be so afraid." I was stunned and thrilled, relieved and excited all at the same time. God had actually spoken to me!

For the remainder of the week I relaxed into doing what I'd been told – liberated by not having to play God or be responsible for outcomes. My job was to love people where they were, assure them of his love and faithfulness, and then provide an opportunity for all of us to chat together (pray). I returned to Cape Town inspired and encouraged that God was indeed alive and working though ordinary people like me in ways I didn't understand. That encounter in 1977 expanded my understanding of faith in an awe-filled way, and set me free to expect and ultimately see God work more powerfully in the years ahead.

It also provided the wellspring of vision and passion that made me want to take the next step toward full-time ministry and serve God for the rest of my life. I submitted to the discernment process and was accepted for training and eventual ordination.

My unexpected sojourn in Oxford arose after a kind and generous mentor offered to pay my airfare from Cape Town having suggested I study overseas. Nothing like that had ever happened to me before; it was too good to be true. Eventually after quite a convoluted process I arrived in Oxford and took up residence sharing a college apartment on Norham Gardens road; one block away from Wycliffe Hall and two minutes' walk from the park.

I meandered around the town in wonder, pinching myself that I was to spend three years in this famous ivory tower of learning. Lichen covered spires rose to the heavens above narrow winding streets, stone walls, manicured lawns in famous colleges, plaques everywhere commemorating the accomplishments of those who'd studied here during the 800 years prior to my arrival.

I relished the prospect of being free from the oppressive political climate in South Africa. Every year there were call up papers from the army to attend three week military training camps that I'd managed to avoid for six years since completing my compulsory service. There were so many emotions. After years of wandering at last I was breaking out of the orphan straitjacket; these three years promised to be a new foundation that I hoped would launch me into a much more positive trajectory for the rest of my life.

Ivory Towers

They exchanged their glorious God for an image of a bull, which eats grass.
They forgot the God who saved them, Who had done great things in Egypt.
Psalm 106: 20-21

Six months passed before God spoke to me again.

Studies were well underway – about three short essays a week discussed in small tutorial groups of three students and one tutor. State your case, defend your argument, and articulate the premises for the chosen line of reasoning. It was intimidating, exhilarating.... and hard work.

Historic churches abound around Oxford and on Sunday morning bells peal across the rooftops and turrets where the gargoyles live. Services are offered to satisfy your spiritual palate – would you prefer traditional worship, contemporary, organ, guitars, Prayer Book, extemporary, or a good mix of all in a liturgical salad? One man's worship is another's blasphemy.

If I'd had a vision of the prostrate figure immobilized on a couch fifteen years later ignoring his two young daughters and choked with disillusionment and depression I'd have gasped in disbelief. These years in Oxford were an unexpected gift and privilege from God in whose hands I'd placed my entire life. I was living and studying in one of the world's greatest academic environments and meeting famous people who inspired my faith and resolve.

I attended St. Aldate's Church across from Tom Tower – Christ Church College. Contemporary in style, Michael Greene was senior pastor (vicar) providing stimulating teaching with a consistent challenge to live Christianity in the market place. "If God is real and Jesus is alive then it'd better be good news for Joe and his wife and three kids."

I met Jackie Pullinger at St. Aldate's and heard how she worked in the Walled City of Hong Kong with chronic drug addicts. She'd already laid down her life for the poor, prayed over countless addicts and witnessed the power of God setting them free – cold turkey. She was a living example of Christianity demonstrating power and transformation - the works of Jesus happening today. *That's what I want*, I thought to myself. *There has to be more to Jesus than choir, church attendance, and not dancing, smoking, or drinking!*

I volunteered when Billy Graham came to town and surprised everyone by turning up at a training session. He shook my hand and thanked me for volunteering. He addressed over 700 Oxford theological students and teachers with remarkable humility speaking simply about the love of God and the power of Jesus and he soared in my estimation.

Another weekend I traveled to London to hear Joni Erickson speak at All Souls, Langham Place. I expected a rather dour presentation from a sad person who'd become a quadriplegic after a tragic diving accident at the age of seventeen. Instead an attractive woman addressed the packed gallery with radiant joy. "I'd rather be in this wheelchair and know Jesus than be healthy and ignorant of Him." I listened in awe and sometimes with tears; I desired her passionate faith. I wanted to spend my life proclaiming the awesome wonders of that kind of God.

Me in Oxford! I'd responded to the call of Jesus and God had blessed me so unexpectedly. I was confident that my education and passion would be welcomed and appreciated when I completed my training and returned to Cape Town.

I walked the streets of Oxford and settled into life in England. I was pumped and God was good.

The evening I heard God's voice again I was somewhat reluctantly attending a joint evening service with another college at Saint Giles on the Woodstock Road. I wasn't excited about the high church Anglican style with robes, bells, incense, and the austere formality.

I sat in the long wooden pew discouraged by the lack of change in my life and wondered how God can forgive again and again? *Do other people here share this ambivalence in their Christian lives?* Of course they did, but we're meant to be preparing for full-time ministry. *Will I ever be spiritual enough, pure enough, or well behaved enough?* Discouraging thoughts pummeled me as I sat in the dark candle-lit church.

To my surprise a gentle stirring arose within me. God's Spirit revealed a truth that ignited the evening, smashed my defeated mentality, and has been a source of hope and inspiration ever since.

My mind wandered back to a few evenings earlier when I'd seen a BBC news clip on television reporting how the Royal Air Force used two old ships for bombing practice. The ships were strategically positioned in deep water of the English Channel and deliberately sunk.

There in the church a 'divine replay' began. I stood beside Jesus on the cliffs of Dover surveying the Channel. He pointed to the two ships floating on the water in the distance, useless hulls potentially dangerous to other shipping if they'd been left drifting free. I can still visualize the dark outlines against the shimmering sea and the easy and friendly conversation he drew me into.

Side by side we watched the aircraft fly overhead and drop their bombs. At first there appeared to be no effect, then one ship listed and the other began to lift her prow high as the ocean poured into the stern. Before long both vessels disappeared beneath the surface. No trace of them ever having floated there was evident, just vast herds of horsetail waves cantering across an empty ocean.

Jesus' voice broke the silence, "John, how long are you going to stand here and wait for those ships to return to the surface?"

"They won't," I replied. Then hesitating I blurted, "With due respect I've just watched them being sunk in deep water, it's impossible."

"If you arrived here now you'd never have known those ships had ever been there would you? Let's go to the bottom of the ocean, and see what's happened to them," Jesus smiled, obviously enjoying the moment.

In a flash we did just that, such is the miracle of the mind and spirit. The ships were no longer dangerous floating chunks of iron. Now, on the ocean floor I saw that they'd been transformed into reefs teeming with an astounding array of sea life. Fish swam and darted everywhere with coral and barnacles and other forms of plants sprouting from every inch of the vessels' surface.

Jesus spoke to my spirit. "John, when you offer me something, or ask me for forgiveness, I want you to know that I receive whatever you give me as surely and completely as these ships sank into the ocean today," He continued, "Whatever you entrust to me is taken forever and will never surface again in my memory, nor should they arise as doubts in your heart and mind either. Take note of what's happened because this is what transformation looks like.

When those ships sank they filled with water and they sank into water. In other words water and ships became one - ocean into ship and ship into the ocean. The result was that something wonderful took place, a miracle happened. That which was useless and dangerous was transformed into a reef offering shelter and life where a multitude of creatures thrive."

I sat silently in the pew, oblivious to my surroundings, completely transfixed by the revelation.

"Why am I telling you this?" Jesus continued, "Because I want you to know that I take every negative, all the mistakes and rebellion in your life and I recycle them into new life-giving gifts that will bless you and those around you. If you entrust them to me I'll perform the miracle every time, I love recycling," he smiled. "I can transform anything that is ugly, dangerous, useless, and poisonous, into something beautiful and enriching for you and for others."

This was the Jesus I loved and whose voice made my hair stand on end. He was neither religious nor aloof. He reassured me that in all my incompleteness, my internal struggles, and my self-doubt he would continue to release and renew. "If I can transform a wreck into a reef surely I can do the same in you." I'd return to this moment many times when I was overwhelmed by my unworthiness or discouraged. The message was always the same; "Trust me with you."

The image faded like a hologram and I was back in the church, a thunderous organ accompanied the first hymn, and incense filled the air. My heart was pounding as hope abounded, my surroundings melted into the background.

During the rest of the service I replayed the scene in my mind - inspired, encouraged, and alive to the love and tenderness of a God who met me even where I didn't want to be – amidst ritual and religion. It was here and at a couple of other times in my twenties that I discerned the meaning and call on my life most profoundly; when God broke through the austerity of religion, penetrating my confused solitary journeying, and loved me like a father. I never ceased marveling that he saw me and heard me in the hidden places of my heart. And that he accepted me in my incompleteness and 'unholy' state.

In my college years sometimes revelation would come through a verse in the Bible, other times the words of a speaker, or perhaps in the midst of worship I'd well up with emotion and feel his presence. Faith would rise - releasing peace and an assurance that my belief in Jesus was not merely theoretical and locked in my head. I didn't mind 'not understanding the experiences' as my heart often took me to places my thoughts could not enter. It was in these times I "knew that I knew" God's touch. It was deeply meaningful and evoked a response.

This was what I wanted to grow in and help others encounter – for the rest of my days. Nothing else came close to the life he brings.

Those breakthroughs convinced me that God never intended for me to be distant and cerebral with him. He wanted to share experiences with me that significantly impacted my lifestyle while inviting me to use my brain and engage with academic theology and reason as much I wanted to. The important point was to appreciate that my personal relationship with him was my source of passion and inspiration.

When the door opened for me to study in Oxford I was convinced he'd made it possible, as it was beyond my dreams or expectations. He spoiled me with a generosity I'd not known and filled the gap my father never knew how to bridge.

That's why, when years later I lay on the couch following the affair, I was so broken. It seemed as if he'd abandoned me because of my misguided choices. I had little appreciation at the time of the ruthless nature and role of spiritual attack that will expose and exploit any character flaw it can possibly sink its teeth into. Unbelief and ignorance regarding the power and presence of evil works in its favor much like the absence of sterilization in early medicine actually increased the probability of infection.

But on that couch my anger was directed at God. Despite all that I'd done for him and how faithful I'd been, he seemed to ignore me and be impotent to heal, protect, or transform. All my pleading appeared to have no impact. The fall shattered my career, my life, and everyone around me; and God didn't seem to care.

Dead Man Walking

*I am overwhelmed with troubles and my life draws near to death.
I am counted among those who go down to the pit; I am like one without strength. I am set apart with the dead, like the slain who lie in the grave, whom you remember no more, who are cut off from your care.*
Psalm. 88:3-5

Four weeks after Christmas I slouch among nameless people at the Vancouver Airport terminal awaiting my flight to Toronto, it's January 1997. I stare blankly. Hollow numbness presses me into the seat. Tears reservoir against the back of my eyes, one bump and they'll cascade into the open.

I'm a dead man walking.

Arriving in Toronto, I booked into the hotel at midday and headed for the conference - within walking distance. The air was cold, snow on the ground, wind sharply lashing exposed skin. It was a Christian leader's conference and I was hanging onto my 'leader' identity by my fingernails. This was my last gasping cry to God, heaving desperation from a hollow shell of unbelief.

I reclined (collapsed) along the back row of chairs, eyes closed and screamed – at the same time hoping no one would come too close.

"*Talk to me!*"

"*God, please,*" I begged. "*Let someone come and give me a prophetic word of hope!*"

And still I could not let anyone see my shame or comprehend the turmoil I was struggling to articulate.

As worship began I heard a joyful and enthusiastic response roll toward me from the stage. I lay alone, bleeding, angry, like the man beaten by thieves and dumped beside the Jericho Road, the religious people passing him by. Unable to endure another second waiting for a Samaritan or a miracle, I fled. I booked an evening flight I couldn't afford and returned dejectedly back to Vancouver.

It would be many years before I attended another Christian conference.

In the local ministerial, only one person reached out to me. All others were distant and silent. Intellectually, I understood. What could they do? How do you approach someone who's guilty of an affair - no matter the rationale; especially when he's not very receptive?

I knew the response people desired regarding my behavior. But the unmet emotional need handcuffed me in the dark. And no one could see it.

The previous month I'd wasted countless hours immobilized on the couch, the size of a coffin. It wasn't long before Christmas but nothing sparkled that festive season; I was deaf to joy and blind to good news. I withdrew into myself, gave my bright young daughters perfunctory hugs, and tried to immerse myself in art.

I burned portraits as I'd done years ago; faces with weathered features from around the world tattooed with a heated point into wood and rendered golden yellow shades of brown with linseed oil when complete. I began experimenting with watercolors and learning the challenges of working with colors and light through many hours of trial and error. I didn't have to think - which made the activity a distraction without demands.

On Christmas day I drove alone to Ucluelet and Tofino on the West Coast of Vancouver Island while Karin and the children went to church and tried to celebrate Christmas dinner with friends. I can only imagine the pain and humiliation she was enduring as she stoically tried to hold everything together while I was tearing it apart.

Fresh snow covered the side of the road and trees as I drove westward under heavy skies. I stopped to photograph an eagle perched high in a gnarled cedar surveying the surroundings, maybe I'd attempt to paint it in the future. I fantasized about becoming an artist where I didn't have to deal with people on a regular basis. Photography in the back of my mind was about capturing and composing images through the lens to paint.

An hour later I turned left at the fork in the road and ordered egg and bacon at a nondescript diner in Ucluelet. Plastic tablecloths with cheap salt and pepper shakers, holly leaves and spray-on-snow proclaimed the festive season in the windows. The sound and smell of deep fried bacon and eggs accompanied the local radio station blaring nauseating Christmas jingles. A few scruffy others who probably had nowhere to go either hunched over tables sipping weak coffee splashed into bottomless white cups by a disheveled waitress.

I wasn't celebrating anything that day. I was hiding, cringing in a cave stripped of every ounce of dignity, confidence, or hope. I was no better than my fellow diners. I was participating in their 'church' which superficially looked very different but really wasn't. While Jesus was born I was killing time and cursing the existence of this day that pronounced good news and great joy – what a joke! I felt a sarcastic anger simmering within. God seemed as impotent in my life as the Father Christmas figurine decorating the windowsill symbolized the distribution of gifts but gave nothing.

I walked the grey beach under a grey sky occasionally staring out across a grey sea; hands buried deep in my jacket pockets. I wondered where she was and how she was doing. I shook away the thought but it clung like lint to Velcro then pulled over for more coffee before heading back. Loneliness and despair were passengers all the way, refusing to get out the car despite my protestations. I was reduced to a reluctant chauffeur empty of any sense of a final destination. I couldn't bring myself to make a U-turn and meekly return to the status quo of my previous life where I failed to anticipate much empathy or understanding.

Had I known this was the beginning of seven years of torment in a hell of depression and isolation, would I have turned around?

Shortly after the disastrous trip to Toronto I paced the floor of the rustic cabin on Saltspring Island – where the dreams had once glowed so radiant and bright. Now they were scattered shards littering the ground. I'd snatch a book only to cast it aside before a page had been read. I'd pick up the guitar but there was no song in me. I'd walk around the property but the stunning view was bleak and blurred. I looked at the car and checked in the small storage shed for duct tape. I found a roll and spotted the hose lying stretched like a snake through the long grass. I could easily connect it to the exhaust pipe and place a brick on the accelerator. Everything could be over in ten minutes. No one would find me for days. All pain would vanish with a few gulps of carbon monoxide, the humiliation, fear, desperation, all gone. The gnawing futility that never left me...

I sat and stared out the window for hours contemplating death. I saw my daughters' faces with blonde hair and impish grins, seven and five years old. I imagined their smiles fading slowly and breaking into horror and tears at the news of my death. I considered the years ahead of them without a father.

I would be crippling them with the very curse that had orphaned me.

I hurled the roll of duct tape across the room. "I'll do life on my terms.... I want to be free! The first love that had once exploded in my heart and filled my spirit to overflowing had evaporated."

And yet, there was enough life left to make me step back from the ledge.

I looked out of the window toward the distant mountains of Vancouver. "I'll find another trail where Catherine walks and follow the footprints there," my heart declared. "There's no way you can get away with that and you know it," my mind retorted. I was imprisoned.

The truth was I'd no idea where to go; besides she wouldn't come with me anyway.

Thoughts of suicide continued to appear with alarming appeal.

One evening Karin called my friend and doctor who graciously visited me with a troubled and bewildered look on his face. We'd played squash together, often joked around; but not tonight. He tried to talk sense into me; I was unable to provide him with what he wanted.

"I don't know where I'm going," I said, head in hands staring at the carpet. How could he understand or condone my heart being torn apart? I felt stupid and helpless, childish and aching with longing and despair.

"Would you try an anti-depressant, it may help to take the edge off your highs and lows," he suggested. "It'll give you time to regain some balance."

"Alright, I'll grab hold of anything right now."

I sat in the rocking chair, lay on the couch, tried to read, enveloped in a cocoon of silence. I described my inner despair and turmoil in the lines I pecked out into raw poetry every day. As I trudged through the heavy mud of daily darkness and despair writing was a safety valve that helped relieve some of the internal buildup of pressure. Poetry was an easier medium with which to capture feelings and emotions. It erupted – a gushing flow of words, roughhewn, crudely formed, and caked in the stench of decay, self-pity, and depression.

Initially I wrote for myself and for those closest to me as a means of expressing what was going on inside. It was self-absorbed and bleak, tough to read and even harder to live. What do you do with someone in such a gloomy place when they have no idea what to do with themselves?

Validation was the elusive Holy Grail to my psyche and soul. What I wanted was someone to say they understood, or at least to appreciate my inner turmoil. But I couldn't accept anyone who tried because it seemed no one would listen without attempting to fix me. So writing became my safer place to express my desperation and understand the traumatic confusion.

The words poured out on pages every day. I dredged the turmoil within; all my disappointments, anger, and unmet longings screamed in a cacophony. I had no idea I'd lost the guidance and meaning in my life. My eyes were transfixed on the circumstances around me, the pain it was causing, and the seeming lifelong series of betrayals. My inner dialogue offered evidence of my worthlessness and God's lack of love – "You're as silent as the dead and obviously don't care at all, I wouldn't respond to my children like this." Within my distorted paradigm rejection and despair was a logical conclusion. Where the spirit had failed skin had to suffice, and another woman had become the object of my desire and allegiance.

Except I was still trying to do the honorable thing in my marriage and calling as a pastor, which meant somehow ignoring these confused feelings and longings and hoping that merely expressing them would make them eventually go away.

Around Easter I returned to work with the desperate prayer that I'd reclaim what had been lost. I figured if I was busy again, it might help. But ministry demands the whole person. And unfortunately, I was empty.

"It's so nice to have you back John," a church member said, greeting me after my first service back. "I trust you're feeling better."

"Thanks," I replied with a weak smile, "Hopefully we're moving in the right direction." My words echoed against the cracked canyon of my heart, I felt like a balloon with a puncture, deflating and heading down, bracing for the inevitable catastrophe.

I never desired to live a double life nor did I intend to continue as a pastor hiding a secret. The antidepressants helped but nothing had really changed. Karin and I still could not connect with one another.

"What can I do?" Karin asked, tears welling in her eyes. She was used to making diagnoses and giving prescriptions. This vague nothingness from me was excruciating. She tried to take my wood burnings to an art shop on Saltspring to encourage me but they weren't up-market enough for their clientele. I felt sorry for myself and for her, and yet had no clue how to let her in. I worried about what would happen to her. Time would reveal that she was far more capable of navigating the chaos than I.

She'd embrace me. "Can't we sort this out and make it work?" she asked, kissing me on the lips.

"I really don't know."

I hated how unhelpful I felt.

I lived on the edge of a chasm. I'd call Catherine but couldn't, or wouldn't, let go. She never initiated; it was I who pursued and needed the listening ear. She felt guilty. "I don't know how to walk away or reject you," she confessed.

"Why don't we just run away?" I said.

"Oh, yeah, where would we go? Besides we have children to think of."

"Well everything's so screwed up now…" I thought. "I have no idea how to keep going. I can't see where I'm heading …"

"I'll never abandon you," she promised.

Thus, even over the phone, I came alive. We were two lost damaged souls, locked in a tortuous death spiral that would last seven years. I couldn't let her go, believing it could work while she felt the shame of being responsible for my disgrace.

As I disintegrated in a very public arena, juicy gossip and finger pointing followed the salacious news of my downfall. And my cries for help were inaudible, "What about me? What am I supposed to do?"

After four months back at the church I stood before the congregation and announced my resignation. I surveyed the sea of faces, people whom I loved, the closest and most supportive family I'd ever known. They had welcomed us into their hearts when we arrived from Cape Town. Our children were born in this community, some were their godparents and many were close friends. Twelve years of our lives had been shared here.

"I'm so terribly sorry that I've failed and betrayed you, Karin, my children, and everyone I know. The truth is I have no idea where this chaos is leading; the only integrity I can display right now is to step aside and protect you – from me."

I walked out of the door into confusion and desolation, leaving behind those experiencing the same. The road ahead was unfathomable. I drove down to the inlet and walked through the trees along its bank totally numb.. Part of me was relieved that at last I could disappear and hide, another part was frightened. There was no family to turn to and all of my friends were in the church community I'd just left. I couldn't expect them to be there for me as they were hurting and probably angry as well. How could they choose between Karin and me?

I watched a fishing boat head toward the ocean. Its Canadian flag tugged in the breeze and gulls circled in its churning wake. Failure and hopelessness draped over me like a heavy cloak. The maple leaves were beginning to tumble to the ground in fluttering gold, reds and browns rendering the branches as nakedly exposed as I felt.

The following week I sat alone with a pile of cards and notes from members of the church expressing love and gratitude for what I'd given them over the years:

I thank God very often for sending you to us......I will be ever grateful... I have come to a closer relationship with Jesus...You are a gifted teacher ....my life is changed....

The cards blurred before my eyes as I read them through tears of confusion and a ravaged heart. I was the rotten apple in a basket full of fruit shaking a fist at God. *Why me? Why does it have to end like this, to be publicly humiliated, heartbroken over a deeply personal disaster? Why couldn't I be content with what I had?*

A few days later Karin and I agreed to separate while I worked out my life. It wasn't a long conversation. I called Lindsay my friend who lived alone on the other side of town. He said I could camp in his basement for a while and I piled some belongings together amidst the oppressive silence.

At the door, I faced the puzzled hurt in my daughters' eyes. I leaned over to kiss them goodbye and saw a pain that still haunts me. "Daddy's going away for a while... I choked out." Michelle was five years old. Her eyes retreated down a dark tunnel inside her. I knew the trauma I was causing would cut deep - but what else could I do?

The broken bewilderment on Karin's face merely exacerbated my shame; I threw my bags in the car, sat behind the wheel and sobbed. I drove away as the world I knew disintegrated around me. That night I lay in a sleeping bag on a thin foam mattress and hardly slept.

Now what?

The Dark Side Of The Moon

But they soon forgot what he had done and did not wait for his plan to unfold. In the desert they gave in to their cravings; In the wilderness they put God to the test. So he gave them what they asked for....
Psalm 106:13-15

The days were slow and lonely.

I hid in the basement realizing that all the hard work that had been poured into building a vibrant multi-generational Christian community was gone – for me. The void inside and the sense of emptiness was immense. All I wanted to do was be with her because she empathized and understood me.

Some people who meant well left me books to read with exhortations to make 'Christian' choices and do the right thing. My response was white-hot anger fired with expletives because I didn't know how to do that. From my perspective it was like being told to rise up and walk on quicksand, which would apparently magically solidify when I applied positive thinking. Instead I retreated even more.

That's when the 'affair' really began; two people finding solace in an intensity of emotional fault-lines splitting far behind and deep into personal histories. Catherine and I began to meet again. Now there was no more to lose. Upstairs in Lindsay's house I'd hear laughter every night as he chatted on the phone to Diane his fiancée. They were to be married in a few months and normally I'd have joyfully conducted the wedding. This was to be a wonderful answer to prayer for both of them – cries from their hearts for God to give them everything I'd sabotaged and walked away from.

There was little joy in that basement as I pondered my future, which was every bit as bleak as the encroaching fall weather. Catherine and I desperately clung to one another in the midst of chaos. I was paralyzed; I couldn't go back to Karin because I felt so misunderstood, and Catherine and I couldn't move forward because our situation was so clearly wrong according to Christian teaching (which we agreed with).

Anger surfaced – at God, the Church, and my father. I knew that I was never returning to be involved with a church ever again. I was the gossip of the town so there was no way anything would work out there anyway. The anti-depressants blunted the edges off my highs and lows enough to dull my senses. I drank gallons of coffee and gazed vacantly out of the window during long empty days. I visited the government offices and filled in the application for Unemployment Assistance as a 44-year-old out of work pastor.

I'd hit the bottom hard, a bleak plateau on the dark side of the moon where I'd wander for years; much longer than I ever anticipated.

I was scared, floating out of context, adrift with no point of reference or safe harbor. Cut loose from church and God I headed in another direction.

"I gave you everything I had," I railed at God as I walked out the door. "I submitted to your Church and poured my heart and soul into it, and for what? I did a hundred good things with almost zero impact and when I try to be understood, all hell breaks loose and nothing's left. You don't seem to give a shit. I'm nothing but a joke."

If depression is anger turned inward, I was there, feeding the dark monster within. I repeated this mantra again and again, "I'm so bloody sick of the Church, politics, whining Christians and their petty complaining – that's what's killed me, not the supposed terrible pagan world 'out there!'" Rage, self-pity, and blaming melded into a formidable alliance – irrational and illogical perhaps, but honest, finally. And when I discovered Catherine shared a similar reality, well, there was no stopping us.

My sole comfort was a small inheritance from my father's estate that enabled me to be self-supporting for about one year. "How ironic," I thought, "Dad was hardly there and now he helps keep me alive."

I needed to relocate as Port Alberni was too small and my fall from grace was blathered all over town. Anyway I intended to continue the illicit relationship and some anonymity would be welcome. "God can't be trusted and putting him and the church first hasn't worked," I muttered repeatedly, "So what does it matter anymore, can it get any worse?"

One evening I was spending time with the girls and the phone rang. I answered, "Hello?" Silence. "Hello?" No one spoke. I replaced the receiver and checked who'd called; it was someone I'd known for many years who couldn't bring themselves to talk to me.

I went back to the girls but I seethed inside. I could understand people's disappointment and even awkwardness, but to be treated like a leper or judged without discussion? There's no way to express my deep feelings of injustice in words. The intensity of my anger, the deep-rooted disappointment with God's apparent indifference and silence, and the hypocritical distancing of those whom I knew had secrets of their own.

More than once I walked past a fellow pastor in the shopping mall and they looked the other way rather than stop and converse. To be fair I'm not sure I'd have been too interested or engaging myself. Yet this was my continual experience and it only deepened the wound.

I was aimlessly flicking channels on Lindsay's TV one morning when Guy called.

"Hi John, Guy here, I wondered how you're doing and whether we might have coffee some time?"

Guy had travelled quite a journey himself having lost a successful business through poor decisions and even worse counsel. It had knocked him right out of the ballpark into bankruptcy and he was ever so slowly beginning to pick himself up as a business consultant. He'd relocated to Port Alberni and joined our church community for support on the long road back to stability.

"Sure, that would be nice," I responded. "I don't get many calls these days."

"So how's it going, I imagine life is pretty tough right now," Guy said peering through black-framed glasses over his mug of coffee. Dressed in charcoal trousers, red cashmere sweater, and thick black hair beginning to fade to grey he looked like a distinguished and In fact he was a few years younger than I but his image and demeanor served him well.

"It's not easy," I replied, looking around hoping no-one I knew would walk into the coffee shop. "I'm not sure what to do or where to go."

"I know the feeling," Guy responded. "I remember wandering around the island wondering what to do and having to start knocking on doors again. To be honest we're not out of the woods yet."

"What I hate about this is that when my personal life falls apart I lose everything," I responded ruefully. "I mean I understand why, but what do I do to reinvent myself at 44? I can hardly get out of bed in the morning."

"Why don't you enroll for the course I'm about to facilitate at Malaspina College in Nanaimo?" Guy suggested. "It starts next week and at least is something to do. It'll be covered by UI (Unemployment Insurance) so won't cost you anything?"

It was the first positive suggestion I'd heard in ages. I agreed to give it a try. My back turned defiantly toward God. I'd get on with my life, whatever was left of it, on my own. Catherine was all I had to warm my spirit in my increasingly isolated position. She was also completing courses at the same college so we'd be able to get together there perhaps.

They may as well have named the course 'Back to Square One'. That's how it felt stepping into the modular classroom the following Monday morning. College age kids and a handful of aspiring entrepreneurs attended but I couldn't relate to their optimism and great expectations for a future. I used to love academic environments, the bustle of cafeterias between classes, colorful noticeboards overflowing with events, and even the silence of the libraries.

This time I was the old man, washed up with a secret trying to repair the damage of the past and survive as I edged toward an unknown future. Bill wanted to develop a rap-style clothing brand, Kate had a creative idea for home decorating, and Colin was an underwater photographer – a handful amidst twenty others looking for expertise to build their dreams of becoming self-employed. I had no creative ideas, no visionary concept to share, nothing exciting to bring to the table...

"Exploring small business and consulting," I responded lamely – when asked.

Driving back from the college one day with Guy I mentioned that I needed a place to live. "Have you tried the resorts?" Guy asked. "They have cottages they manage and rent over the winter months". My heart leaped at the suggestion, "That's a great idea," I replied.

We pulled in at a resort with summer cottages lining the shore. Guy's car idled in the parking lot as I walked through a thick carpet of leaves to reception.

I inquired with the woman at the desk. "For how long?" she replied.

"I'm not sure," I hated to explain. "I'm going through a difficult time and need some space." I knew I presented a despairing picture standing at the reception counter empty-handed with lifeless eyes.

"I understand." She smiled empathically. It made me want to cry. "There's a cottage you can have on the beach until next spring, fully furnished."

The price was a little high but my father's inheritance fortunately took the edge off desperation. Guy and I drove down to a tidy two-bedroom cottage on the edge of the beach with a stunning view across to the mountains north of Vancouver. It was ideal with enough room for the children to join me occasionally. A few days later I moved in, stocked up with a few supplies and sat at the table sipping canned soup in silence.

One evening toward the end of the course Guy and I sat in the car and chatted about possibly working together.

"I find this business development quite interesting you know, even though it's a rather different world to what I'm used to," I said. "It's funny, even in the lectures during the day I'm expecting to pray and invite God into what we're doing and then I remember that's the wrong context. I'm angry and sort of rejecting him but still notice his absence, strange isn't it? What are you planning after this is done?"

Guy sipped the coffee from the mug that seemed permanently stuck to his hand, "I'm trying to drum up some consulting work in the area and have a few leads right now."

"Do you think there's any potential for us working together?" I asked somewhat tentatively. "I sure need help; perhaps our different personalities could be a strong combination."

"Funny you should say that, I've been thinking the same thing," Guy replied with a grin. "I know of offices that may be available and wanted to take a look at them. I couldn't guarantee what the monthly income will be, but it's worth a shot."

"That would be wonderful," I responded. "I've my inheritance to help for a while….."

It was dark when we parked in the maple-lined road in Parksville where Guy thought we could rent some office space. Fluorescent lights flooded the entrance as we climbed the stairs to look around and meet the landlord. The business environment was alien territory, nothing sat easy or familiar; perhaps I was sleepwalking through a bad dream and would soon wake up. Memories of my first job in an advertising agency office as a young nineteen year old resurfaced, I'd no more confidence or clue what to do now than I had back then.

We rented two small offices and Marketplace Group Consulting was born. Fortunately Guy knew the ropes well and methodically steered us forward landing small contracts that barely kept us afloat. More often than not we were scraping the bottom.

I trailed along helping on business plans, hosting sales workshops for small business owners, and helping others reinvent themselves.

Guy came into the office every morning coffee in hand. He made calls and networked effortlessly. I sat in my small office staring at the blank wall behind an empty desk formatting the occasional brochure and feeling useless. I searched the internet and the news about a manhunt on Everest which was underway. One of the first to attempt to reach the summit the man disappeared without a trace in 1924. Now someone had found his body almost perfectly preserved – he'd slipped and fallen from the North Face and laid there frozen for 75 years.

I had a degree in psychology, virtually two in theology from prestigious universities, years of practical experience in counseling, teaching, and leading an organization and I was sitting there looking at the picture of Mallory's marble white back frozen on the mountain. At least he had died doing what he loved.

I glanced at my watch. "Another two hours." I rolled back my chair and walked across the hallway, leaned against the doorframe and waited for Guy to finish his call. I envied his obvious delight and comfort in the consulting world, but I had to admit I didn't think I'd ever find fulfillment there.

Torn Apart

...but they mingled with the nations and adopted their customs. They worshiped their idols, which became a snare to them. They sacrificed their sons and their daughters to false gods.
Psalm 106: 35-37

My daughters loved me unconditionally and their hugs and smiles were life-giving to my troubled spirit. When I was with them the world seemed easier. I envied Karin having them at home as company to help fill empty and painful hours. She had the church community to comfort and support her through these excruciating months as well as the familiar routine of her medical practice. My bright light in the dreary weeks came with the opportunity to spend time with the girls.

Sometimes I brought them to the cottage overnight and we played in the swimming pool, watched movies, and went for walks on the beach. After I dropped them home I'd often return choked with emotion as I drove back into the void.

"I wish they could live with me, life seems so much better with them around," I mused. "But I can't afford that…. My income's so small, sometimes only a few hundred dollars a month." Then I'd cycle through the litany of life being unfair, the inequality between Karin and myself, my fear of the future, and hopeless resignation.

I was passively allowing a solid family and a secure life trickle through my fingers. My inability to clench a fist and fight left me resigned to watch it all slip away.

I knew a huge source of anger and frustration was the abandonment of my calling as a pastor. It's one career where the job was inextricably intertwined with my core values and beliefs, stimulating and fulfilling. Yet for that very reason, when a single element faltered the entire structure collapsed. And for me, that included the loss of God for support and comfort as my faith melted under the heat of accusation and guilt. My sin was obvious. Consequently the only solution was my termination as a pastor, which I agreed with. Except, given the nature of the emotional "crime," I felt I'd lost far more than what should reasonably be expected. Every muscle had collapsed and I had no strength left to fight. What I knew I should do I couldn't, and even God seemed to be a distant observer.

In the absence of a better answer, I gave up expecting, hoping, or even asking for assistance.

How do I reinvent myself while in the midst of isolation and personal despair? I'd heard many stories of deadbeat dads and wasn't planning to join them even though my finances over the next few years hovered virtually below the poverty line.

Everything was gone and I'd caused it because of the unmet and unresolved turmoil inside of me. True or not that's how it felt from my vantage point. Political correctness, Christian values, peer pressure and expected conformity, or at the very least having the courage to work out commitments honorably and faithfully. My head intellectually applauded the very sentiments that my heart, for the first time in its life refused to submit to.

I assumed everyone around me was sharply focused on my betrayal, adultery and unfaithfulness, my irresponsibility and my personal failure. I ached for the shoulder of a parent to lean into and the chance to tell the story of years of emotional wandering without a home. I wasn't looking for approval but understanding as to why it was hurting inside – that was all. As I drove back to my cottage by the frigid ocean I fantasized about wading out into the darkness through the surf one night and never coming back.

I entertained the prospect of relocating to the cottage on Saltspring Island. I researched buying a small gift store; perhaps I'd fit into the artist community and re-emerge in the laid back island culture where anything goes and few questions are asked. After a few days I felt too isolated and gave up. Reality was I had no energy to initiate, or commit to such a plan.

Almost every day I'd walk the windswept shoreline wondering where I'd be at this time next year, or in five years' time. I'd regress to emotions I thought I'd left behind a long time ago, only now discovering they'd lain dormant mere inches beneath the surface; feelings of abandonment, being a loser, and the unfairness of life.

"Why is God so absent and the negative so powerful?" I yelled on the beach; then thoughts of Catherine's presence, her words, and her body tugged me once again to seek her out and quell my frenetic despair. I'd meet with her far less frequently than I would have liked, but those were moments of brief reprieve when the inner turmoil found rest.

Over the next eight months Guy and I pecked away at small contracts in the workplace scraping together a semblance of a business. I lived in the beach cottage spending many long hours alone. Though I relished my time with her I felt ongoing ambivalence with Catherine where guilt, children, and the everyday challenge of staying alive took its toll. Neither of us were at ease either pursuing nor ending things.

Every Wednesday and Saturday I would drive over to Port Alberni to see the children. Karin was gracious about my visiting the house as we'd agreed to try as best we could to keep life as normal as possible for them. She'd take the opportunity to go out and our exchanges were usually respectful. We never called each other names, raised our voices, or deliberately set out to hurt each other.

"You've got what you want so why aren't you happy?" Karin asked during one of our brief conversations. I'm not sure how I replied but it was obvious we were not hearing one another. She'd given some ultimatums if we were ever going to reconcile and I decided to try again.

From my perspective, it seemed that Karin could not comprehend or consider any underlying cause that would explain even some of my actions. She stoically continued with her life and from mutual friends I knew that she shared much of her pain and devastation with them. My betrayal shook her world to the core and it is undoubtedly one of my deepest regrets. But my fear on returning was that what had felt like an oasis of understanding and nurture from Catherine would be lost forever. I'd be revisiting a desert wasteland or be required to endure months of counseling until I was fixed.

Catherine felt similarly trapped and agonized over her three children as well as the perpetual shame laced with anger over unresolved and unacknowledged issues with her husband. We both had taken our Christian commitment seriously and what we were doing went against everything we believed in; which was why the situation could not continue.

The decision to make the change was the hardest I'd ever made in my life – to do the right thing. I packed my meager possessions from the cottage to head back 'home', said goodbye to Catherine and we went our separate ways with no plans to meet in the future.

I couldn't live with myself without at least trying to repair the damage my actions and decisions had caused. Karin's parents were visiting from South Africa. Their presence was a support and profound blessing to her and represented so much that I felt I didn't have. No matter how much they may have loved me and welcomed me it was not the same as blood ties.

They were much loved by the community in Port Alberni after having spent a couple of summers with us. Karin's mother was quiet and stoic, always encouraging and supportive in the background, astute and careful with her words. Her father was a strong conservative Christian, eager to lend a practical hand wherever he could but with a temper that flared up when challenged. His daughter could do no wrong in his eyes.

In the months since I'd left the church Karin naturally questioned her sense of self. She sought affirmation and comfort in an affair with a long-time mutual friend of ours who was married and lived in Arizona. They met up on a number of occasions. I questioned her about the friendship that no one else knew about, including her family.

"What's the difference between what I did and what you're doing?" I asked as we talked over the counter in the kitchen one evening when I was visiting the girls. They were occupied in another part of the house.

"I can understand your anger," I continued. "But I lost everything as a result of my actions. You seem able to carry on with no consequences"

"It's different," she said.

"Do the girls know about Todd?" I asked

"No, of course not," she replied.

"Is this relationship going somewhere, does Alison know?"

"No, – it would be devastating. Yes, he'd like to take it further but I can't see that happening," Karin replied.

"Yet you fail to comprehend why I get angry at the double-standard? That I can say I understand why you have gone down that road but you can't see why I ended up with Catherine?"

"You betrayed our marriage first, it's not the same," she said.

"You felt rejected by me and betrayed by your friend," I protested. "Can't you understand I also acted out of unresolved pain as well? It's not all about you but family and childhood, struggles in the Anglican Church, and abandonment with my dad? Those realities for me don't appear to be valid or important to you. I need someone to care and listen... I'm not saying my actions were right at all but...."

I'd thought that Karin seeking solace in the company of another woman's husband would perhaps provide a bridge of empathy and understanding between us.

"It's different; I didn't cheat on you...."

I put on a brave face as I returned 'home' because I felt both guilty and responsible. I'd concluded that no explanation or excuse from me would ever be acceptable. The bottom line was that I'd broken a marriage vow. Returning home was my way of laying down my life and doing the right thing with the hope and prayer that positive change might follow at a deeper level. Karin received emotional support from family, church and work. Mine was negligible.

The day after my 'return' Karin, the girls, and her parents left to tour the West Coast of America for four weeks. I always seemed to be watching people leave.

I repainted the house and wondered whether Karin had any idea what I was trying to do. Irrationally I mused, *"If she wanted to rescue our marriage she could've forfeited the road trip. Everything's always on her terms. Nobody will ever understand what it's taken to walk away from Catherine and come back to make amends."* I sounded like a pathetic broken record in my head. The problem was I didn't know how to shut it off.

Wrapped up in my struggles I couldn't appreciate Karin's side, having to deal with my rejection and betrayal. All I could see was the support network for her and the absence of any around me. I was aware that she was in two minds and wasn't finished sorting through her behaviors and resolving some of her survival patterns.

Neither of us had much idea how to cope so we bumbled along. In my self-pitying martyrdom I constantly felt as if I had to give up more or do something else, while Karin called the shots. She was understandably reticent to believe much had changed.

"Is it really over with Catherine or do you just want to return to the security my income offers you?" she asked.

"Yes it's over," I replied desperately wanting to believe my words. "She's going back to Peter to see if they can work things out and I'm not continuing any contact, I promise you."

"Well I'm not sure I'm ready to try again, but I guess there's nothing much I can do about it now," Karin shrugged.

I was sleeping downstairs in the guest room the following night when Karin appeared at the door. She snuggled into my bed and we made love that felt like a tender homecoming. "I never thought we'd be here again," she whispered. "Nor me," I replied. For a few months hope flickered while I plodded through mundane consulting projects and Karin visited South Africa, ran the New York marathon and continued her medical practice.

Every few weeks we trekked over to Vancouver for counseling sessions but somewhere a cord had been broken by my betrayal that proved impossible to repair. We both had many personal issues to resolve; and too often trying to understand each other ended in frustrated exhaustion. I'd written over one hundred pages of poetry describing what was happening inside and I gave it to the counselor during one session. She asked, "Is there anything more you want to talk about, John?"

I answered with tears in my eyes. "I've written and communicated more than most about what I'm wrestling with and my inner turmoil. I have nothing left to say that would make any difference." Through the mist of my blind heartache I had no emotional energy to reach out to Karin any longer.

"What about you?" she asked turning to Karin.

"I know what he wants but I can't give it to him," she replied. I wanted her to get out of her chair and embrace me, to accept me as I was. I never felt she truly wanted to understand me, no doubt because she felt the very same way.

The shutter fell and I gave up. The only way I could stay in the marriage would be to completely acquiesce and die inside. Karin's sense of betrayal and my abandonment filled the room and asphyxiated us. More counsel would only have destroyed any remaining common ground.

Our attempts to resolve our pain had led to vastly different consequences. I broke first from our lack of relational fulfillment. As a result, she got to maintain her lucrative career and the financial upper hand. I'd worked six days a week for fourteen years, but it meant nothing – and the despair, impotence, and injustice fed my depression and kept the darkness thick around me. And now I was virtually penniless.

I enrolled for a Master's degree in an attempt to do something worthwhile in the midst of what seemed like a long plunge into a bottomless valley. When I left for the three-week summer residency, both of us knew we'd reached the end.

The weeks in residence were a welcome break from the threadbare consulting grind. I was hollow inside and trudged through the leadership program with little passion or excitement. I befriended Jenny, a mother of three in the midst of a disintegrating marriage and we spent hours walking through the campus talking. I was an empathic ear and she gave me welcome attention.

Jenny was a teacher and one of the most optimistic people I've ever met. But our age difference and backgrounds soon made it clear that we couldn't sustain the brief relationship and she ended it.

I walked the beach in bitter despair once again.

Anger was never entirely absent. I would have nothing to do with God and his apparent silence cut deep.

My life revolved around work, squash, and endless drives to coffee shops and bookstores killing time and seeking the anonymous company of strangers. I sat alone in pubs and restaurants reading the newspaper trying desperately to stay alive and not be tugged down by despair's dark tentacles.

I joined the local squash league and it became my refuge and church. No questions were asked and no judgment given. People were friendly, offering an easy camaraderie as we played our league games and shared a pint or two afterwards. There were no expectations or demands placed upon me, something I had not known for twenty years. Conversation was superficial, which for a while at least was fine by me; I was weary of the deep.

Two years had passed when I called Catherine somewhat nervously from my office - she was continuing to struggle in her marriage. One rainy night I waited for her to finish work and we embraced in a car park. It felt good. After years of testing ourselves apart, perhaps we were destined to be together after all. I should never have made that phone call – it may have saved at least one marriage. Instead Catherine and I embarked on another skittish dance of intimacy sabotaging any chance of lasting fulfilment.

On her side there was always some reason for not stepping into a future together. I kept hoping that over time circumstances would settle down and I took seriously my responsibility for causing some of her struggles. I willingly provided her with significant financial support for years but she always felt a huge weight of responsibility for my downfall and couldn't shake the curse of illegitimacy over our relationship. If anyone had integrity between us it was her. I was the one who insisted we could make it.

My assumed identity as a businessman mirrored my disastrous social life. Slowly I learned how to reframe my background as a pastor into Human Resources lingo: marketing, 'No need to sell, just help people buy', team-building, motivation, leveraging, attending to the bottom line, features and benefits, productivity and outcomes. I joked that marketing God in a hostile market on the West Coast was much more challenging than selling software products.

For two long years I lived in a small apartment with walls and ceiling so thin an Exacto knife could have sliced through them. Frustration, apathy, fear, and a growing sense of desperation were driving me insane, my life an aimless dinghy drifting in a vast ocean. From my balcony I could see the mainland across the Strait. In the summer, a flower seller brightened up the lawn across the road with her radiant blooms plunged in white buckets under a white tent. I wondered what it would be like to feel hope and expectation again. But the color and beauty only deepened my sense of isolation.

One evening I vainly attempted to smoke a joint. Nothing happened. Another evening I sat alone gulping bottles of beer and wine wondering whether intoxication would help. A few hours later I knelt in the washroom and in-between heaving spasms was adamant that this was not a path I would stumble down or a throne before which I would ever bow again.

Karin filed for divorce into our third year of separation, which I had no energy or inclination to contest. I reluctantly relinquished the Saltspring property as Karin agreed to purchase my portion, there was no way I could afford to keep it and build a new life. It was an agonizing decision but the circumstances forced my hand. It was the only way to access the capital to finance a three-acre lot I found not far out of town with an old cabin and a sizeable workshop. "Large treed acreage and beautiful rustic cabin" the advertisement read.

It was exactly what I needed; something to work on. The cabin renovation would become one of the most significant factors helping me out of my lingering depression and aimless existence. I had something to do, dream about, and invest in. It was a means to an unknown end.

All the while, I continued to ignore God. If he was going to be indifferent so would I. I feigned a lack of care but my anger would rise and snap if challenged or provoked. I couldn't shake the victim mentality and the ongoing battle for financial stability that shrouded my life like a dark curse. In retrospect, I blamed him for leaving me stranded.

Ripping apart boards and planning for structural changes gave me a semblance of accomplishment and control. Later the restoration would provide a bridge and a metaphor promising a brighter future. When I spent my first night alone amongst tall cedars beneath the moss covered shake roof I couldn't see that far.

There was a much longer road out of this hell still ahead.

Trading Spaces

We look for light, but all is darkness; for brightness, but we walk in deep shadows. Like the blind we grope along the wall, feeling our way like people without eyes. At midday we stumble as if it were twilight; among the strong, we are like the dead.
Isaiah 59:9-10

"Where do I begin?" I mused… sitting in the sparsely furnished cabin rocking in the dilapidated wingback chair that migrated with me. I'd moved my few belongings across from the apartment earlier that day; bits and pieces providing a thread of consistency from here back to that insecure childhood in South Africa. My grandmother's beaten copper coal scuttle, side tables I remember in her home when I was a boy, two oil paintings – one of a Cape Dutch house and another of mountains glowing under an incandescent setting sun.

It was early spring, a time of new beginnings, more daylight, and increasing warmth. Although not yet, this year spring showed up still shivering providing a perfect excuse to build a fire in the woodstove and begin to dream. The cabin was what realtors describe as having "great potential", "a handyman's dream". The thick shake roof was at the end of its life, the small washroom had already been diagnosed with rotting joists, while the kitchen consisted of little more than a stove, a cantankerous old fridge, a small sink, a few cupboards and a red linoleum countertop along one wall. At night I could hear the mice scurrying across the ceiling.

Outside the kitchen window a large cedar draped tired branches over the cabin surrounded by foliage that encroached into what was once a large clearing. A red cedar hot tub with a broken heating system and crumbling floor leaned against a small elevated porch where an empty bird-feeding platform was nailed to the corner railing. Dampness left its moist breath hanging in the air and on the walls; dancing room for light was hard to find.

I failed to appreciate the symbolism of the cabin on arrival although I knew escaping from the apartment was a breakthrough of sorts. Next to the cabin was a large workshop where a boat builder refurbished the interior of sailboats that neighbors told me used to be "moored" at the top of the driveway. The dark teak doors throughout the cabin boasted of his handiwork and the oiled cedar-lined bathroom replete with brass fixtures may once have been cozy but now it was dark and damp.

I met Jamie through an advert in the local paper and a recommendation. Grey and bearded, eyes wrinkled at the edges, dirty truck, and a pleasant disposition was enough for me to like him. We negotiated a mutually sweet deal for him to work the three acres and clear some ground, selectively log marketable fir and cedar, and complete rudimentary landscaping.

Over the next few weeks Jamie disappeared into the bush with his chainsaw and giant trees crashed to the ground as he carefully logged, cut, and piled the wood in the driveway to be hauled away. His battered Caterpillar heaped debris high for burning and scraped the ground into flat surfaces for planting. In no time light poured in, spaces opened up, and we could see the sky. His twinkling eyes, "can do" attitude and easy familiarity with the land cheered me and I was sad to see him leave.

I began work on the small washroom, dismantling the existing fixtures and plumbing, opening an exterior wall and replacing the rotting joists. Fortunately I was alone as I prefer to figure these projects out as I go along. My plan was to salvage and recycle as much material as possible and then rebuild in a West Coast style.

I'd begun messing around with wood when I arrived in Canada, building furniture, beds, and minor renovations in the rectory in Port Alberni. At Saltspring I'd become more adventurous, making the new property somewhat habitable with an outhouse, a small log cabin, gazebo, storage shed and deck. It was my way of planting roots and settling –perhaps a nesting and a yearning for a home.

I build rustic primarily because it's more forgiving and requires less stress. I've never been a perfectionist and prefer to be creative and unconventional at times. The fact that my newly acquired property was within one of the last remaining regions where building permits were not required was a priceless bonus.

A squash-playing friend of mine, Neil, was a longhaired scrawny fellow and a local jack-of-all-trades construction man. One day he visited at my request, after surveying the cabin we discussed the potential. Another afternoon he sat on my couch, steaming coffee at hand. Looking out the window his face broke into a huge smile and he cursed. "Why don't we build large windows with a rising roof line that will give a perfect view of the forest? Like this...?" he explained sketching his revelation on a scrap of paper.

"Sounds good to me, let's do it!" We planned the process of removing a wall, pouring foundations, and raising the roof. Neil would build and frame and I'd dismantle what needed to be removed and prepare the site.

Though I was still floundering with work and my personal life, having something to do was a giant step forward in combating my despondency. I'd no idea where I was going but renovating and building helped contain some of the emptiness and kept despair at bay. At least I was accomplishing something when tearing up a floor and hammering nails.

It happened every subsequent year in the workshop without fail, but the first time was a surprise when I opened the door. Suddenly there was a fluttering of wings and a small blue-tinted bird was frantically flapping up and down pressed against the windowpane. It's trapped, can't get out, little heart beating like a drum through its feathered chest. As I approached with hands outstretched it tried feebly to escape. My fingers closed firm and tight over the exquisite blue-grey wings.... "I'm going to set you free," I whispered, "No need to be frightened." I tenderly stroked its head; beady eyes stared, lost and bewildered as we stepped outside into the forest. I slowly raised my arms, opened my hands, and released the fragile bird to rise with a swoop and swirl into the trees.

God, I feel so trapped. I've lost touch with love and freedom and am stuck against the glass frantically flapping... it's terrifying, lonely, and exhausting. Everything I'm involved in seems cursed and hard work with minimal reward – socially and at work.

During one of the breaks with Catherine I sat at the squash club nursing a beer…Billy Joel's 'Piano Man' should have been playing … *'the regular crowd shuffles in… there's an old man sitting next to me, making love to his tonic and gin… sing us a song you're the piano man….'*

That's when Susan and I conversed late into the night. She was a member of the club with a reputation for drinking. But this was the month she and a few others made a pact to abstain. We talked about our lives and some of the pain she lived with. Deep sorrow over a broken marriage and divorce from a man she evidently still loved.

"Why are you crying?" I asked peering across the table in the dimmed light.

"It's nothing," she replied.

"I used to do this for a living Susan; I can recognize pain you know."

She proceeded to share about a family member who had been permanently injured when in their early twenties and how she still felt responsible. She'd visited them in Vancouver earlier in the week so the reality and memory was rubbing fresh and raw.

"Thanks for listening," she said as we left that night. "Wanna come to dinner on Friday?"

"Sure," I replied, "Sounds good, will be nice to have company."

Once again my rudderless boat ventured out in search of love, or something that I wasn't sure how to find and we struck up a lonely friendship that lasted for nearly a year. I learned that coffee laced with vodka was not obvious to the uninitiated and witnessed firsthand the cruel grip of alcoholism.

More than once Susan staggered into my house at 2 am under the influence of prescription medication laced with alcohol.

"What are you doing here?" I asked, "How did you drive like this?"

Wanted to see you honey?" she slurred with a grin, "I'm still kinda cute aren't I?"

I held her by the shoulders to keep her from falling and raised my fist - I was so angry. I felt manipulated and at my wits end. How do I get out of this? God my life's in turmoil. I could understand how people lose it in utter frustration and helplessness. I lowered my hand and steered her toward the bed. There's no way I could send her out in such a state. Within minutes she was fast asleep with a smile on her face while I lay fuming.

I remembered how easily I dispensed advice to others. Now in the midst of my muddled life good choices and rational decisions were few and far between. God was still an observer in a faraway land. The conversation would surface every now and then around the table at the squash club. I'd argue and debate for his existence, ending with a disclaimer, "I believe in God and could introduce you to Jesus; I'm just not talking to him myself right now."

I said the same thing to Susan and gave her a Gospel of John. "Read this," I said, "It's easy to understand. You need help with this drinking; I can't do it for you."

"I need support, if you'll come with me to AA I'll go," she replied.

I couldn't say yes; it would mean committing to the relationship that I knew wasn't going anywhere. And then I had this bizarre thought, "If I ever return to ministry Susan would never understand or fit in." I'd no intention of doing such a thing but the words stuck in my head nevertheless; I couldn't imagine ever going back. But nothing so far had fulfilled me either.

By now Guy and I were working with a software company helping them penetrate the North American market. Fourteen months earlier we'd left our consulting endeavors for what appeared to be a great opportunity. Guy's business experience was precisely what the company needed and my background fitted well with the vision of building a strong team atmosphere. However as time passed tensions began to rise with the entrepreneurial owner who wrongly perceived us as a threat to his 'kingdom' and was making sounds of wanting to pull the plug on our agreement.

On the bright side the girls and I spent a wonderful three weeks in the southern hemisphere; my first glimpse of life and a measure of joy in five years! This was the break that would finally end my destructive detour with Susan.

En route to New Zealand we stopped for five days in the Cook Islands where white sandy beaches fringed with lush green vegetation and coconut palms merged with turquoise seas. Before making the trip the girls and I completed a scuba diving course with the intent to dive there. I joked that it was a great activity for a father and his teenage daughters, "Fit them with gear, send them underwater with a breathing apparatus in their mouths and we have peace on earth."

We rented equipment and were ferried out beyond the reef that encircles much of the island. Rolling backwards over the side of the aluminum boat we sank into crystal clear water where visibility was at least one hundred feet. The coral reef spread out below in various shades and shapes of white and cream formations. Every now and then we turned to one another giving the 'ok' sign before continuing to explore this wonderful world. Colorful fish of all shapes and sizes darted back and forth, resplendent with every color of the rainbow. We watched our air bubbles float up through the azure water to pierce the dancing glass ceiling far above. What a wonderful world – indeed!.

New Zealand reminded me of my childhood in South Africa with Victorian buildings in the suburbs of Auckland, miles of beaches, and cricket; a sport that Canadians cannot comprehend. We spent two weeks visiting my brother and his family, drove down to view the colorful hot springs at Rotarua, and imagined ourselves to be in the land of the Hobbits amidst undulating green hills. I played golf, and we tubed through an underground river – what a surprise.

Two hours' drive from Rotarua we discovered the Waitomo Caves where The Black River Rafting Company offers guided tours through spectacular underwater caves. We donned wetsuits and followed our guide to a cavity in the rocks on a mountain slope that gave no hint of the treasure within.

"You scared Michelle?" I asked as we walked down the pathway. "No way, this is cool," she replied with a grin scrambling to be first in line. Clutching inner tubes we slid and jumped into the black water below gasping as the cold water seeped into our wetsuits. The darkness was pushed back by lamps on our heads illuminating spectacular formations of limestone. We floated through caves with high ceilings lit by hundreds of little stars (actually the fluorescent excrement of worms) – beauty in the strangest of places from the most unlikely sources.

Above ground we relished the long sandy beaches drenched in sunshine day after day after day. We spent a day cruising aboard a tall mast sailing boat, lying in the netting, hanging over the bow, riding the waves and getting soaked with spray. It melted me on the inside – enough to experience the faintest zephyr of fresh air, tugging at the cobwebs and disturbing the dust of the depression that had settled over the years. After clawing and clinging to the edge of existence for what seemed like an eternity it was a reminder that there were better places to be alive.

The return flight to Vancouver Island was a long journey back to uncertainty and reality; to an undefined business future and the need to extricate myself yet again from another abortive 'friendship'. Airplanes are ideal places for reflection – 30,000 feet above ground and in-between places.

"Who would have thought?" was a repetitive phrase within my psyche as I considered what had transpired. I'd been so confident, faith-filled, and clear about who I was, where I was going, and what my life's purpose was when I studied in Oxford. I wanted to serve God, share his love and hope with people and build communities who could encourage and support one another along the way.

Perhaps the warning signs of pending danger ahead were flashing at my ordination?

I closed my eyes and leaned back in the seat, the girls were plugged into movies and music; we were somewhere over the Pacific Ocean after dinner had been served. My thoughts rolled back to the beginning of my 'career' as a priest – a term I'd never been comfortable with and tended to avoid. I saw the mountains and vineyards of Stellenbosch where I'd walked twenty years ago with a dog whose name I never knew.

Man Of God

Help, Lord, for no one is faithful anymore; those who are loyal have vanished from the human race. Everyone lies to their neighbor; they flatter with their lips but harbor deception in their hearts.
Psalm 12: 1-2

I plucked a stick from the ground and tossed it down the farm road where it ricocheted off a fence post onto the dusty gravel road. The boisterous farm dog bounded after it and returned with a huge hound-grin and a furiously wagging tail. We played and strolled through the surrounding vineyards exploding with greenery. The valley dipped down to the whitewashed farmhouse and rose beyond to the cobalt sky. It was late spring when the fruit begins to bud and swell. The slapping rhythm of an irrigation sprinkler accompanied the panting dog and the sight of a dripping scarecrow made me laugh; he looked as if he'd had a night on the town and the last thing he needed was a cold shower.

"Thanks for being here," I said, "You've saved my life." I held the dog's head in my hands and stared into large brown eyes blinking behind a wet nose. He tried to lick me and I pushed him away ruffling his ears. "What on earth am I doing here buddy? I'm not sure I'm really cut out for this kind of life. God, seriously, is this really your will and purpose for me?" I stood up and threw the stick one more time, my four-legged confidant joyfully chased after it quite unaware of the gift he was to me that morning.

I was 28 years old, just completed a Certificate of Theology at Oxford, unmarried, and about to begin full time ministry as an Anglican priest.

The days preceding ordination to the priesthood commonly include a retreat where time is spent in reflection, prayer, and reading. I longed for ordinary people to walk alongside me and chat, question, encourage, and interact with. Instead, I'd submitted to convention as a sign of obedience.

I embarked on a solitary drive through wine country to the picturesque town of Stellenbosch situated among vineyards and mountains outside Cape Town where kind people with a beautiful farm made their guesthouse available. There, I was subjected to a monastic solitude except for periodic visits from the local priest who was overseeing my retreat and long walks with a dog.

Many Christian pastors and clergy have a strange way of "being holy", when their ordinary persona is intentionally subdued and someone else emerges in the "role of priest/pastor". In their view God is very serious and solemn, and communicating with him has to be structured, using words others have written, and seldom with much joy. To me, it was incredibly boring. I couldn't understand why a personal God would not want us to talk to him from our hearts in an authentic unscripted manner.

It was here that I felt panic rising at what I was getting into. I wanted to scream as I imagined slipping into an institutional straitjacket. I was confused about the meaning of being humble, submissive, and a servant; I consequently shoved my gut-feeling aside and endured the process. I'm sad to say conversations with my retreat leader amounted to little more than sharing formal communion each day and his making sure I had no unconfessed sins lurking about.

Only weeks earlier I'd returned to Cape Town after three years in England. I'd been appointed to a suburban church as an assistant priest to a man I had little in common with and a tradition more formal than I'd ever encountered. The required interview with the Archbishop (whom I had not met before) was austere; similar in tone to meeting with a headmaster or a dignitary, both of which, at least functionally, he was. Three years earlier in this same office I'd enthusiastically said yes to follow Jesus into full-time ministry. Now that I was 'ready to go', the institution took over brushing aside any true warmth and comfort or a touch from a humble servant's hand.

I suppose we've always been a rather odd couple – the Anglican Church and me. While I tended to be more casual and friendly, she preferred a formal and dignified relationship with the Deity. I'd grown up thinking of her as "the church" and therefore her ways defined for me what it meant to "be Christian". I wanted to serve God but not really like this. Nevertheless I was accustomed to her ways. To exclude her from the conversation would feel awkward even though she was stifling and often embarrassing. I see an uncomfortable similarity to people who report remaining in an abusive situation for so long – it's simply all you know.

Perhaps the seeds of the depression to come were sprouting back in that vineyard as I reluctantly allowed myself to be squeezed into a mold that somewhere inside I knew would never fit. I wanted to follow Jesus, be his servant and share his common touch and unthreatening friendship. When first welcomed after expressing an interest in full time ministry I was assured the church could use people like me. However those reassurances were lost when the men who had said those things moved on or had retired by the time I returned from my studies. Religion, tradition, and procedure were firmly established. I'd come too far to turn back and lacked the confidence to stop, re-assess and perhaps find another route. Instead of acknowledging a sense of 'being out of place' I reframed the situation into my needing to submit to authority and trust God anyway.

Weeds of anger and frustration would quietly grow around me over the years, sprouting thorns of resentment at being misunderstood and unappreciated. As my true self was continually sidelined or simply tolerated the gnawing irritation would eventually cause me to snap. I had a great rapport with the common parishioners but inside the institution I was kept at arm's length and regarded as "difficult".

The church was busy at the front lines - as it should be, challenging the South African government regarding the injustices of apartheid. Yet its internal life and leadership largely ruled out any questioning of traditions. That which Jesus shared with all - personal touch, the revelation of God being for us, not against us, a Father and a friend in relationship, was an abstract concept in most churches.

My orphan spirit failed to find help or nurture in the impersonal mannerisms of clerics, administrators, and people simply *doing their job*.

Constantly denying what I intuitively knew settled into my bones like a cancer and pressed down before finally metastasizing many years later.

When I visited Ron, the Priest at St. Savior's Anglican Church in Cape Town, I hadn't yet learned the difference between submitting to God and submitting to a church tradition. It so happened that my parents had been married there, the imposing stone structure full of history with its traditional graveyard nestled in the shadow of the mountain.

He was a lanky bespectacled man with grey hair and trousers always too short. In his somewhat droll British accent he shared his love for tradition, ritual and Anglicanism.

"So you've just returned from Oxford I believe," Ron said with a smile that reminded me of the wolf masquerading as Red Riding Hood.

"Wycliffe Hall," I replied.

"I'm a Cambridge man, but I'm sure we'll get along just fine," he snorted before outlining the workings of the church. My heart sank behind a faint smile. Right there I knew I'd been drafted into a church too formal for my spirit that longed for contemporary freedom. My greatest encouragement was that God had lived among ordinary people in the person of Jesus – and I wanted to do the same. The longer he spoke of prayer books, liturgy, and robed processions the more firm my sense of what life in a clerical bubble would hold for me. Similar to what I imagine an arranged marriage must be like; I as the bride stifled my gasp of panic and gulped hard.

This was going to be tough work.

I totally underestimated the power of bureaucracy and the politics within established church traditions, hierarchy, and disciplines.

My appointment to Ron's church was as a freshly minted priest fulfilling a function – personality, passion, and giftings came a distant second to the prescribed needs of Mother Church. In England those with whom I trained spent weekends away at interviews as they shared the discernment process regarding their first placements. In Cape Town this decision was made for me "in the interests of the Church."

I suppose I shouldn't have been surprised either that the religious formality around my ordination encapsulated almost everything I chafed against. It was as if I'd said 'yes' in blue jeans and after the completion of training the cookie cutter went into action in the name of tradition, Anglicanism, and conformity.

Pomp and ceremony, robes of all shapes and colors, incense, the 'us and them' processions where priests paraded and everyone else watched. The overpowering organ music, austere songs followed by recited prayers. I wondered why it made anyone more spiritual to heighten the formality and read the same old thing to God every time. Particularly when Jesus came to break the religious formalism he encountered in the synagogues of his day?

Dressing up and standing on pedestals is an occupational hazard across the broad spectrum of the church. A smooth-speaking orator in a packed auditorium with his or her brand name ministry, technology everywhere, bands and coiffured choirs can be an equally religious production.

In one of my earliest recollections of church (I was about five years old) we accompanied my father to St. Paul's in Rondebosch, Cape Town. The warm rusty and yellow sandstone building was imposing. Walking through the arched doors I was unsure whether I was entering a palace or a castle.

Inside soaring buttresses and beams lift a peaked roof to the heavens. The windows rise majestically and stained-glass scenes loomed large.

I can picture the procession passing by as if it was yesterday wondering when it will end.

The words read told of Jesus who was humble and easy to come close to. One who loved children and whose depiction sculpted above our heads in radiant colors cared for people. Boys and girls were perched upon His knee and a lamb was cradled in His arms. No fear or distance there. Instead I felt I'd entered the guardhouse of a King who was very distant and serious and the guards/clergy would determine who came in, when and how.

"Excuse me sir," the hostess tapped me on the shoulder, "Please keep your leg out of the aisle, I nearly tripped and you wouldn't want someone's dinner spilled over you I'm sure," she smiled.

"Of course, I'm sorry," I replied hastily tucking my foot under the seat. These hostesses have such patience I thought, and are so diplomatic. Sometimes I find I'm moved almost to tears by the smallest of gestures of kindness or consideration from another. Glancing down the row my daughters snuggled into their seats fast asleep. My father's heart delighted in the weeks we'd shared together. I hadn't felt such joy in a long while.

Over the years I'd learned that God's love can also rage fierce and strong like a father when his children are threatened. And I remembered when my heart beat in rhythm with that courageous warrior whom I followed in the midst of protests in Cape Town.

As a teen and young adult in South Africa I joined in rallies where thousands gathered and police mingled with guns drawn, dogs straining leashes, and tear gas filling the air. Though it was terrifying it was also exhilarating - believing so strongly and standing so firm.

The issues were deep and hard to grapple with: *What does it mean to passively resist an immoral regime? How do you love an enemy who relentlessly harasses and oppresses you? When is it time to act rather than pray or reason? What does a just society look like and how can we be part of the solution?*

I participated in this demand for social justice in the streets as a young priest and was proud of the church identifying injustice, declaring God's passion for the poor and disenfranchised, and doing something. I marched to the Cape Town parliament buildings next to Bishop Desmond Tutu until rows of helmeted police, shields, guns, and dogs prevented us from getting too close. My heart was in my mouth but my spirit cried out to God, "There has to be change in this land! Please don't let them shoot!"

Sometimes I, and others, would volunteer to spend the night in the house of a clergyman living in the townships outside Cape Town because of the fear of Security Police raiding in the early hours of the morning. I worked in a church where the police would frequently gather outside our house across from the school for 'Black' children. The police deliberately taunted them to come out and then chased them around the streets with long whips (sjamboks). If I went outside with a camera the sad truth was in those days a White face helped as some sort of deterrent.

But I discovered that the same courage and resolve to help individuals encounter the love of Jesus and his power to transform and heal was absent. It was missing in church congregations, as a core value for clergy interpersonal relationships, and in the ability of the

Anglican Church as an employer to care for those who labored under her umbrella. The straitjacket I'd so feared being trapped in slowly did its work. While addressing the socio-political environment was safe and full of opportunity, encouraging a personal spiritual life was largely apologetic, insecure, politically correct and lacking relational warmth, passion or intimacy.

While my enthusiasm for declaring the relevance of Jesus touched the lives of those in my local congregation, in the wider church I was tolerated and sidelined. The anger and hurt gradually turned inward to infect the still weeping wound of childhood alienation and a distant father. I was like an irrigation pump where people came to drink while beneath the surface my supply was beginning to run dry.

As with religion, depression preys on the confused and vulnerable, and it had dogged me for so long since my fall from grace. I was once a relatively energetic and sociable person with a smile and wit that could come to the fore amidst a gathering of friends. I loved music and would often play the guitar and sing in times of worship. But my guitar had gathered dust for four years (there was no music inside to draw upon) and for longer than that I'd lived in the shade that encircles depression. This trip to New Zealand seemed to pierce the outer fringes of those shadows; and now for the first time in years I discerned some edges where the light might break through.

I tapped the screen in front of me. The graphic displaying our journey positioned the plane in an arc above the ocean with the North American continent at last coming into view. Maybe four hours of the flight remained. The girls hadn't stirred. I carefully rescued Michelle's book from the floor and rearranged Carmen's sweater around her shoulders. The cabin was silent, blanketed forms bundled in dreams; a few reading lamps piercing the darkness like stars in the night sky. I wandered up the aisle and stretched. A tired hostess poured me a cup of water and I settled back in my seat.

I placed a cushion by my head and closed my eyes. Sleep was elusive as I continued musing on how I'd seem to shuttle in and out of living my life with God as the major figure. Long before I'd become disillusioned I always loved the hope and purpose-filled life he called me toward, but in practice the dream was crushed underfoot by religion. However I knew that dismissing all religious faith in churches was misguided. I somehow had to make peace with the faulty and fractured world that included a faulty and fractured church. It had always been that way; in the time of Jesus on earth, throughout history, and in my lifetime it was no different.

As Crusoe's footprint implies the presence of someone else in the world who independently pressed their foot into the sand, so the Church is simply an imperfect imprint pointing to the presence of another. Its mere existence throughout much of human history suggests there's probably more to life than that which is accessed through my five senses; no matter that the imprint itself reveals gnarls, corns, blisters, and a severe case of athlete's foot.

Carmen dozed on a pillow against my shoulder while a bleary-eyed Michelle was now engrossed in a movie. Neither was aware that their presence in my life was the biggest thing saving me from total self-destruction. Carmen, tall, sensitive and artistic, hid her pain over the divorce much like I did. Michelle, sociable and gregarious was extremely discerning and sharp, and wonderfully unafraid to speak up and voice her opinion. This trip had been something we'd shared together, and I'd persisted in talking to them about my struggles to validate theirs. I vowed then and there to continue to invest in the two most precious lives in my world.

I tugged on Michelle's arm. "What?" she said removing her earplugs and frowning? "What are you watching?" I asked. "A documentary on how they made Lord of the Rings," she replied turning back to the screen. She didn't like being interrupted.

Instead of checking the movie channel I found myself beginning to recall the story that had unfolded six years earlier.

I beckoned to the stewardess again and requested a drink. "A glass of Merlot would be great, thank you.

Double Standards

"Jerusalem, Jerusalem, you who kill the prophets and stone those sent to you, how often I have longed to gather your children together, as a hen gathers her chicks under her wings, and you were not willing.
Matthew 23:37

Nearly two decades before the girls and I journeyed to New Zealand I'd landed in Canada to begin a new life. The irony was that while I was delighted to escape the oppressive political atmosphere and uncertainty of South Africa I soon discovered another challenge amidst the peace and relative tranquility of Vancouver Island.

For the next twelve years I was Senior Pastor of St. Alban's Anglican Church. I'd stated that I was not interested in maintaining Anglicanism (form and tradition) but was enthusiastic about building relationships with Jesus as the focus in a contemporary Christian culture. "That's what we want as well," they declared as they offered me the position. I'd been thrilled at the opportunity God had given my wife and I to begin a new life in a beautiful and peaceful country.

As we grappled with change not everyone was enthusiastic. The organist stormed out after my first service in response to being asked to play one song on the piano. Over the next year the choir was replaced with a music group to lead worship, and books handed out to those arriving for a service were packed away in favor of overhead slides and less liturgical reading. "Why would we ask a blue collar town where people don't read much to learn our rituals in order to understand the message," we asked ourselves. "Let's meet them where they are and make it easier for them to access our community."

The result was that the diehard traditionalists left for "the other Anglican church" while a host of new people were attracted to the more relaxed and friendly atmosphere. There was room to question, groups to join, and God's presence was very real in our gatherings. We were probably one of the most vibrant Anglican churches on the Island, growing in numbers and financial giving every year.

Initially I decided to invest in building the local church, "Let that speak for itself rather than me be critical and negative," I thought. But after about eight years such a posture was becoming untenable.

I realized the Anglican Church in Canada was in a desperate condition. It was fervently cheering those opposing apartheid ten thousand miles away, but the lack of engagement in a fast changing world was strangling life at home. I sat in meetings with clergy who were aware of local challenges and was alternately confused, saddened, and angered at what I heard.

"My people aren't very comfortable with rocking the boat, besides we like the bishop and enjoyed his last visit," said one.

"I only have 8 years until retirement," said another tucking away a smile. "Too much to lose now, I admire your passion John, but I guess we grow weary."

"We've always been more traditional," coughed another who always appeared nervously apologetic. "We adapt to change slowly and - well, most of these issues don't really touch us out here to be honest."

I imagine a similar apathy and indifference has challenged every age (resisting Wilberforce, Bonhoeffer, or Martin Luther King for example) as succeeding generations settle into their respective levels of comfort.

Clergy loyalty to political correctness complicated and often smothered each issue that was introduced at local and general meetings. Discussion was strictly controlled and those speaking were unused to allowing emotion or personal faith to color their exchanges. The office of priest emasculated individual personality, and symbolism squashed substance. The church was intimidated in the face of public opinion. It had little or nothing to say about social issues or anything truly positive about Jesus' public agenda either for that matter. But the major topic of contention was the vexing issue of homosexuality – and it still is to this day, in fact.

Every few years the regional Anglican Churches would meet in a Synod – where matters relating to the church, life and ministry could have an opportunity to be discussed and reviewed – or not.

"Why is it?" I asked from the floor of the Synod facing about 150 clergy, bishops and laity from around the Island, "That if I challenge someone else's opinion about homosexuality I'm labeled as homophobic? I happen to disagree …. We've already decided twice before that homosexual practice is not consistent with traditional Christian belief. Yet we keep advocating more study and discussion; as if the only acceptable answer will be 'yes' to our approving of that motion and thereby agreeing to re-interpret the Bible?"

My comments were met with a smattering of applause, followed with a line-up to the microphone offering further remarks, positions, and pleas for compassion. Eventually the procedural experts herded the topic into a corner with the suggestion, "that we table this matter and request the doctrinal committee to formulate a study guide for churches to use in ongoing conversations on this delicate matter."

Back in my seat, I fumed. *"The cowards can't even make a stand on their home turf."* I was never advocating intolerance or hating and discarding those wrestling with gender identity, all I was pleading for was the right to express another point of view and conviction.

The avoidance, dishonesty, posturing, and religious politics slowly worked on me, dissolving my passion; like being kissed by Judas the impersonal and unyielding process left me feeling double-crossed.

Over the years I discovered that my idealism and hope regarding the integrity of the church and the courageous conviction of those who professed to serve Jesus was by and large romantic.

Like many before me I'd launched in pursuit of God with passion and idealism, but gradually I was ground down by the machine that is religion. And like many, I would eventually compromise and settle into an adulterous affair justifying my duplicity with the feeling of being betrayed by others. I was not alone. A host of other mistresses worked to seduce the innocents… workaholism, pet ideologies, personal comforts, career advancement, even bible teaching ministries.

Eventually we could take what we perceived to be hypocrisy no more and our vibrant church (St. Alban's) of about 230 voted to disaffiliate from the Anglican church of Canada in 1996. I was summoned to meet with the bishop.

The bishop settled back in his chair stroking one hand over the other as if caressing a pet lizard. He was Fagin "reviewing the situation" in Dickens' *Oliver*; his purple shirt dazzled behind a large cross draped around his neck. A small man, balding, shoulders hunched and legs crossed, his black shoes gleamed.

"Hello John, thank you for meeting with me, I'm naturally very concerned about the situation before us."

"So am I," I replied. "I don't know how to explain or make sense of the Anglican Church's stance on sexuality, the authority of Scripture, or even the revelation of God as Father." I'd repeated these questions countless times and knew that this meeting was likely to be our last with no answer of substance forthcoming.

"These are challenging times," he said flicking his pen against his knuckles, "We must be careful not to judge; in such delicate matters we need more time for study and consultation," he continued with a patronizing intonation.

"What more is there to study?" I questioned, "I have no idea what to say to members of our congregation when they read statements in the newspaper from the Anglican Church that invariably are stuck on human sexuality."

"Well John, not everyone agrees with you. Jesus was compassionate and inclusive, extending his love and mercy to all human beings. Isn't that what we're trying to do in these latter years of the 20th century?" He swiveled slowly back and forth on his chair as he stared back at me through lenses reflecting the dimming afternoon light.

"Inclusiveness doesn't mean ignoring behavior and the betrayal of Biblical norms," I replied. "When you visited St. Alban's a few weeks ago people came away so frustrated at your unwillingness to provide any clear answers."

"That's because maybe there aren't any. I'm consulting with my brother bishops at present, I'm sorry your people feel that way."

There was nowhere to go and no bridge between us to support hope for a future that we could share with integrity.

The final outcome of our meeting was that the bishop revoked my ordination papers and cut me loose; I wanted to lean across the table and punch his lights out. Instead I drove home fuming.

I'd naively thought that if we followed due process our request to disaffiliate would be reluctantly accepted. Instead, the Church, using lawyers to unearth loopholes in the paperwork, changed the locks, seized our property and forced us to vacate the premises. The congregation had built and paid for the building and had been established in the community for over sixty years. In the end bureaucracy trumped all.

"The Anglican Church of Canada owns all title deeds," the defense attorney firmly asserted. With the flourish of a signature the matter was decided.

I shuddered as the flames of anger rose in me at the memory even now hurtling homeward through the early morning sky dawning vibrant outside the Boeing's window.

At the time I recalled witnessing the demolition of squatter camps on the sand dunes outside Cape Town. The Anglican injustice had felt so similar. Though *this* violence was meted out with sophisticated legalities clouded in feigned politeness, it effectively quashed rebellion.

I remembered a phrase from that final meeting. "I regret that I have no alternative if you insist on doing this." The words hung with choking thickness over the proceedings as the Bishop terminated our relationship.

Does religion inevitably resort to any means at hand to maintain its grip on power?

In any church many human things can hide beneath the holy. Men and women make careers of church work – as I myself was in danger of doing for a while – which frequently undermines their availability to the call of God. Of course the church is not the only place where this is played out.

I've attended all manner of Christian conferences and events across wide denominational lines. Much there has been good, honest, and sincere. But the presence of ego, greed, and duplicity has been frequently noticeable as well. Human pride seems to observe no boundaries.

Two years later, as I lay in the ditch, fury pouring out of me like drain water, I recalled it all as if it was yesterday. "I'm not the only one who's betrayed a covenant relationship," I whined. "Look at the church." I shook my fist at God. "It's not bloody fair!" I railed with furious words that vaporized in the air around me, heard by no-one. My anger turned inward continuing to enflame despondency. Accusations and betrayal spun in my head like a not-so-merry-go-round carrying my wife, the church, my father, and me in a never-ending spiral of despair.

I savored the last mouthful of wine, placed the glass on the folding table before me and traced the rim with my finger.

I'd blamed the church for being so traditionally stuck and relationally rigid. I'd blamed my past and my family for not providing nurture or encouragement. I'd blamed God for forgetting his promises to bless. There's a grumbling Gollum inside me I find immature and embarrassing. I've frequently been unsure what to do with him or how to quiet tantrums. Once so full of faith and anticipation, confident… now?

What was left inside to keep me afloat?

After the property was seized, our church community relocated into the gym of a Catholic school and continued as best we could as a Christian community. But I underestimated the toll it had taken. Some whom I'd considered friends seemed perpetually dissatisfied while others murmured that I was building my own empire. Our first service as an independent church left me exposed and vulnerable – like a tortoise outside its shell. Within the next year the seeds of my betrayal would be sown and in twenty four months my life, marriage, vocation and sense of direction rapidly disintegrated.

I walked to the back of the plane again to stretch my legs before transferring my attention to a movie to halt the rapid decline into morbid introspection. Soon we'd land in Los Angeles, then on to Vancouver, and finally arrive home late that evening …. To a scene I'd never forget.

I'd dropped the girls off at their home and returned to my half-renovated cabin becoming a house – maybe one day it would be home? While I was away I'd arranged for the sheetrock to be completed by a contractor. I opened the front door and a chaotic mess spilled out before my eyes. The contracting job had been finished but apparently no one had thought to use tarps or coverings for the furniture and floors. I stood there speechless for several moments. I couldn't wrap my mind around the lack of consideration for containing the inevitable dust. Eventually I began to laugh. All I could do was begin some rudimentary clean up.

"Does the chaos ever stop?" I questioned the next morning. I sipped a mug of coffee and surveyed the scene in broad daylight. The interior had been transformed into clean lines edging walls and ceiling. The spacious open plan room spilled out through large windows into the forest that seemed to pour back indoors. It was great - apart from the dust caked over everything like a late winter frosting.

Returning to the software company there was no warm welcome, instead a cool directive for me to remain in my office. The owner stood at the door, "We've had consultants from Vancouver spend time reviewing our business plan," he said looking out the window. "We're not sure there's a place for you here anymore."

Even though I was expecting this news I was stunned. We'd merged companies and signed agreements which now obviously counted for nothing. The lawyer would later tell me, "John, you want justice, we deal with legalities. You could spend $30,000 fighting this but I can't promise anything."

"Perhaps it would be better for you to go home and someone will be in touch. We don't want you disturbing the rest of the employees," the owner concluded before scurrying away.

Two days later I was invited to meet the company accountant at the local Dairy Queen. He handed me papers to sign and awkwardly relayed the news of my termination, again stating it was on the advice of consultants who'd reviewed the company and its performance. I shook my head. The messenger across from me professed the ordinary level of sorrow and the excuse that his hands were tied. I liked him, but as is the case with so many, when the pressure is applied self-interest prevails over truth or justice. To be fair he'd warned me months earlier, "Don't mess with the boss, he'll do anything it takes to get rid of you, no matter what your contract might say."

That afternoon I donned my tool belt and began fastening siding around the new front entrance while trying not to panic over my fast collapsing situation – yet again. I'd carefully pried the long cedar boards off the old cabin and stacked them around the garden. I began to measure, cut and fit them while making my best effort to suppress the anxiety and concern about where to go now. "Am I building this to live in or to sell to put food on the table?" The cat indifferently licked a paw and washed his face as I pounded in another nail. "I guess either way it's got to be finished; and this is better than doing nothing."

The refreshment and hope I'd tasted during the holiday in New Zealand had evaporated.

Eventually Guy and I acquired a contract with another software company which lasted a year. It seemed my life and efforts were under a perpetual curse; I detested being asked how I was doing and having to acknowledge what only sounded like self-pity.

Times were tough as my pay check shrunk. Work on the house became more than a casual project. Now I had to finish it in order to access some of the equity I'd already invested. I was living month to month, and apart from the trip to New Zealand seldom had holidays or much time off.

Catherine and I continued an on and off relationship but I somehow never seemed to measure up. We enjoyed great times together and then it would cartwheel into a negative suspicion usually around my questionable motives or commitment. I wanted to shake her at times, "For God's sake we've been through so much let's enjoy this relationship!" It was a rollercoaster which for years I believed would eventually lead to marriage and a happy ending - when she finished her studies, her son left home, or her health improved.

We'd part for a few weeks and then one of us would break the silence. We'd spend time together only for the cycle to repeat itself. Sometimes I'd scratch my head pondering, "What just happened?" I'd often wondered how people endured such volatility but when you're in the middle of a relationship and have invested so much you keep hoping that it will get better – next time.

Naturally I wanted to be successful and make tons of money so I could boast, "Look what I did!" but I lacked the drive to attain such a goal, especially at the expense of others. I wanted every place I worked to be a joy for the employees and I advocated strongly for mutual respect and finding win-win solutions. I was inspired by the stories of Ernest Shackleton and how he valued his teams on expeditions more than personal success.

I recognized emptiness in the God-forsaken business arena that gnawed at my soul. I hated the feeling of being controlled by money or that the pursuit of profit should be my reason for living.

The irony was that I'd decided to pursue life by seeking meaning and fulfillment from external gratification. Whether it was a relationship, my children, trying to build a business, or fixing the house, I desperately tried to control my environment and it wasn't working.

I've been told that I'm very gifted but nothing seemed to work out and my inner lack of fulfillment fed the quiet despondency that seldom left me. In my heart of hearts I knew what was missing but the anger and sense of being betrayed and abandoned by God was hard to shake. However, empty days in toxic business environments over seven years totally failed to nourish my spirit.

Spirit?

I'd neglected it for so long I'd almost forgotten it had a life of its own. It would take another year before breaching the crusty surface of my awareness.

I continued working on the house building a basement bedroom and laundry area above which would be a master bedroom and an en suite washroom. It was a daunting task and by now I'd learned patience and perseverance, grateful for the challenge that kept me occupied.

Checking my computer one afternoon, I read an email from my alma mater. "You're invited to a class reunion." I skimmed the names of those on the list and the years dissolved as the faces of boys I'd grown up with at school paraded through my memory.

"Most of them are probably successful and retired by now," I told myself as I stuffed insulation into the basement wall. "Here I am with years of education and nothing to show for it. Alan and Peter are probably well into their lives of bliss and financial stability and I can hardly pay the mortgage."

"Dear Charles," I wrote later that day, "I'd love to attend but circumstances make it impossible to join you. I wonder if there are others like me who have struggled. One never hears anything but success stories." Of course I knew of some through the years… contemporaries who'd died of drugs, two committed suicide, and who knows what else.

"Hi John, good to hear from you; of course you're not alone… I myself have been through a difficult time in the past ten years…." I read the reply and was reminded again of how easily lies can become my truth if I fail to test them and press back.

But I didn't follow up.

I bought a book or two on plumbing and spent a month working on soldering countless meters of copper pipe. I read how drainage and venting works and perfected the art of walking away when the process was frustrating or I wasn't getting 'it'. Returning later could make such a difference. Problem solving with a tangible outcome was satisfying in contrast to my long fruitless journey through the gloom of despondent loneliness.

Deep down I knew my declaration to God that I was done with him was contrary to my core convictions. I'd angrily tried to arm-wrestle him into feeling sorry for me and was discovering that he merely waits until the bargaining ends. As the realization dawned my spirit 'beeped' out a weary distress signal.

I longed for someone to pick up that call.

Breaking The Logjam

Though you have made me see troubles, many and bitter, you will restore my life again; from the depths of the earth you will again bring me up. You will increase my honor and comfort me once more.
Psalm 71:20-21

Words, words, words.

I wrote lots of words when my circumstances gave me little to rejoice about. I'd spent five years writing, editing, and re-editing a volume of poems and prose describing the inner cesspool of my depression. It was called *"Into Depression and Beyond"*. I wanted to communicate what it was like to 'outsiders' who struggle to comprehend why those in depression don't simply make better choices and 'snap out of it.'

The countless revisions were cathartic until I found myself trying to smooth the edges and make it sound better than it actually was. My attention had shifted to focus more on the art form than the content. Depression was black, hard to live, let alone read about, and the pain was relentless day after day. As the light imperceptibly brightened I had fleeting glimpses of where I'd been and instinctively attempted to "tidy up".

That revelation in itself was an indication to me that perhaps I was moving forward ever so slowly into a better frame of mind and being.

I grew weary of my introspection and self-absorption yet wanted to continue writing. In the midst of my anger and rebellion against God that now simmered at a constant indifference I began to write about how others could come to know him (eventually published by *Harvest* House as *Googling God*). It was a topic I knew and could explain personally without research. Perhaps it was a subconscious cry, although at the time my greater focus was on the therapy it provided, the art form of writing, and the challenge of communicating a perplexing topic in personable language.

Even then, the relational love of God was disconnected from my heart. But the combination of writing, disillusioned business experiences and my thawing inner hunger eventually drew me into a more open space.

The Christian book section in Chapters Indigo Bookstore was a corridor I'd studiously avoided for years. I'd no interest in reading the next revelation of what God was doing in the world. My library was in boxes, some books on indefinite loan to friends. "Take whatever you want," I'd said. "I doubt I'll ever use them again."

It was therefore quite a surprise when I found myself wandering back, wanting to read words of spiritual depth. I hadn't felt like this for many years. I was intrigued at the shift taking place inside, a new yearning to experience change. I recoiled from the multitude of glossy titles offering quick fixes or three steps to victory by authors who appeared to have God on his or her payroll. I didn't want to be shouted at, preached to, or exhorted to raise my hands shouting praises to Jesus. I thirsted for the stillness and anonymity of a quiet place at the back of a church where I could sit quietly, breathe deeply, and whisper, "Here I am Lord, I'm ready to listen…"

I selected a book by Jean Vanier on the Gospel of John and another by Henri Nouwen. Both were Catholic priests whom I knew to be men with depth whose lifestyles added substance to their message. Normally I'd have avoided this path, self-righteously branding it as mystical or stained glass spirituality; too much mystery, and talk of saints and sacraments.

It was their humble caring work with challenged people that was comforting; those who depended on others for survival. I could identify, being fragile and tentative myself; it would not have taken much intoning of spiritual platitudes for me to slam the door again. But these writings were gentle and bore witness to a God who loves with unfathomable compassion, who never breaks a bruised reed – I needed to hear that truth and be helped to receive its healing balm in the deep places I could barely acknowledge yet.

The process was welcome, intimidating, and involved multiple shuffling steps and blind walking. It was a re-birth of trust. But the interminably slow "hatching" was stretching to say the least.

"Lord," I wrote in the journal that I'd begun, *"I'm sensing you calling - drawing me back to yourself; others are excited and have told me so. Most of them have secure jobs and pensions, retirement funds, and easy mortgages. How on earth is this going to work out?!"*

My journal at the time describes the process of awakening in the context of my everyday life. There was no magic wand or easy fix. It was a path to walk one day at a time, sometimes startling and uncomfortably exposed, on other days exhilarating and overflowing with joy and gratitude.

A month or two after my visit to the bookstore I set off for England. I would eventually see with hindsight that this was the tipping point of a teeter-totter, and what was down in my life would gradually rise as everything slowly began to shift to up.

December 2006: A cloudless winter sky in mid-December. I ferried across to the mainland from Vancouver Island on my way to England. My daughter worked on a Christian Community called Lee Abbey in North Devon and I was visiting her after linking up with other family for Christmas.

Transition was in the air. The consulting business ventures had floundered for various reasons (the books I could write about the dog-eat-dog small business entrepreneurs). After the last venture wound down, I recognized the end of that pathway, but wondered. *What do I do now?*

A few days before departing I was interviewed for a job as chaplain to an addiction center catering to people who could afford their substantial treatment. I was willing to cast my net wide and knock on multiple doors in my attempt to find the path ahead. I'm not very good with interviews as I tend to say far too much and I had no high expectations that I would be offered the position.

I knew on the ferry that day there was significance in my journey I needed to allow, that the future would emerge in God's time. The sense of God's *doing something* stirred in the wind.

Christmas was a great celebration. With Lesley and David, my stepsister and her husband the vicar, and their lively family in Chipping Camden in the Cotswolds. A touristy market town where in the old days sheep flooded the main street and weathered buildings of golden sandstone huddled shoulder to shoulder beneath heavy slate roofs buckled against the skyline. Teashops and grocery stores were warm and inviting that wintery afternoon. The butcher in a blue-striped apron carved ribs in his Dickensian bay window; the covered sheep market buttressing the end of the main thoroughfare.

I visited a silversmith whose family boasted fine silver production in the same building for one hundred years. Craftsmen sat on stools, leather bags tacked to their overflowing worktables. Dust and clutter filled the second story room; yellowing bundles of bills dangled from the ceiling.

Lesley's family lived in the vicarage; a converted stable and grander than it sounds across the road from the church with the twelfth century clock tower recording passing hours with peals across the village rooftops. Moss-green gravestones shoved off balance by age surrounded the church; history seeped from every inch of soil no matter where one set foot.

This was an ideal environment to rediscover normalcy within a family, walking, reading, laughing, and conversations over wine and food in the tiny kitchen. I detected a gentle thawing at work within. Before I left we prayed that God would move in his mysterious and gracious love and open up my way. Though honestly, as I said amen I couldn't see how.

I planned to spend the New Year with Carmen at Lee Abbey.

Twenty-five years earlier I'd cautiously driven the same snow-covered Devon hills to a conference in the New Year for those training for ministry in various colleges in England. Scraggy woolly sheep dotted the hills and sometimes wandered across the winding roads wet with winter sleet. In 1979 it had been a refreshing escape from the somewhat musty theological environment of the previous six months.

Later in the year I returned to work on the community during Easter and then for an exhilarating summer. In fact the last time I'd navigated this twisting road I was heading north toward Scotland with Suzanne.

We'd struck up a relationship over the summer that blossomed into romance. Like clicking needles we knitted long chats that grew into a tangled ball of emotions. After a lonely academic year in Oxford it was good to have someone to link arms with and walk.

In the late summer we took a road trip around Scotland but the further we drove the more claustrophobic I felt and by the time Suzanne left me in Oxford I was in turmoil. I sought the council of a pastor at my college. We prayed over my life as I questioned whether I was afraid of commitment. I knew she'd already endured some traumatic relationships and I had no desire to exacerbate her pain. But I couldn't continue the friendship.

For two months following I felt as if my nerve endings were being rubbed raw as I grappled with what seemed to me shameful immaturity. Finally, I wrote Suzanne a letter and slid it into the red post box at Norham Gardens Road, unsettled, but knowing I'd made the right decision.

Driving toward Lee Abbey my spirit stirred; I wondered whether its hibernation was drawing to a close. God whispered, promising, "I'm making all things new, let's start again." I remembered that my first sojourn at Lee Abbey had been preparation for 'ministry'. Maybe this time would mark a restoration and new beginning for the next phase. I had no idea how that would come into being. My visit to Carmen coincided with a New Year house party at Lee Abbey; this was the first Christian event I'd attended for nearly eight years.

The whisper reassured my orphan heart. I didn't know how to move on alone. But I felt excitement that I was catching a whiff of hope before it was visible. God felt near again. He'd not forgotten me after all. A familiar fragrance, and with it the deep longing for home arose – the rebel orphan was exhausted and unable to outrun the relentless pursuit of a Father I never knew cared so much. I wanted to be found, to be caught, to be hoisted on his shoulders and carried home. I yearned to feel safe again and know that I belonged. I had no idea how, when or what the next step would look like, but I wanted to.

It was good to be at Lee Abbey, to visit with my daughter and rediscover the familiar terrain. Looking down the steep rocks to the churning waves from Jenny's Leap and strolling the coastal path to Lytton, wind whipping up the cliffs. I talked to God and re-aligned my will with his. With open heart I welcomed his hand to guide me as I released my grip on anger and grabbed him like a child again. Relief began to sink into my dry ground.

I waited in the lounge for familiar faces from twenty-five years ago to reappear, but only two remained. It was so comfortable and familiar, like a favorite jacket. I chatted with guests in the crowded dining area and over coffee with some of the younger community members. One girl in particular, a friend of Carmen's, was afraid of what lay ahead for her. Years of despair slid from my shoulders as I encouraged her to trust and explore her options.

"Don't rush," I heard myself reassuring her. "Take your time, this is a wonderful place to find healing – why not stay for another year and see what God has for you?"

It caught me by surprise: a revelation! *Yes. This is what I was born to do.* It contradicted my vow, yet at that moment denial was as futile as trying to say no to saving my daughter from drowning.

The turning was exquisitely subtle, so extremely gentle I almost missed it. God plays hide-and-go-seek with us, like a child uncovering his leg out from under the table wanting to be found. At Lee Abbey he touched my heart with the deftness of a surgeon's hand cauterizing my fear and releasing his flow of love and hope that lasted over the next several months.

One wet and windy afternoon I stood on the cliffs beyond the Valley of the Rocks. The pathway threaded high above a restless Bristol Channel where white-foaming waves galloped across to the Welsh shoreline in the distance. I was mesmerized by a solitary tree awkwardly grasping the last of the autumn foliage; weathered dry leaves pinched between gnarled grey branches. And there, barely noticeable, buds were already formed preparing to release the fresh green leaves of summer still four months away. I saw myself and I cried. I hadn't felt buds for years, but now I did. Could spring be on the way for me?

It was almost too much to hope. I had no idea what I'd be doing on my return to Canada, working at the addiction center perhaps? I was nervous, but knew an unfamiliar anticipation within, the realization that God had not abandoned me after all.

I returned home expectant, apprehensive and encouraged. The addiction center selected another applicant so that door was closed. I accepted the news with a tinge of disappointment trusting that another way would be revealed.

I read *Approaching the Heart of Prophecy* by Graham Cooke and stumbled across a phrase about taking opportunities as they open like windows. He said if we don't respond we will walk back into wilderness. And when we return to the next window we'll be having the same conversation with God. I remember feeling so tired of being lost, I wanted to take hold of this scrap of opportunity and tug on it for all it was worth.

I was desperate and hungry to hear God and sensed an inner metamorphosis without being able to put words to it - yet. I heard a voice whispering about my forgotten identity, and in that moment an explosion of revelation enveloped me. And something in me knew nothing in my life would remain the same after that.

Like a starving man discovering food I flipped through the Bible to the familiar story of Peter's betrayal of Jesus after which he ran away into the night in despair. "I will follow you anywhere," he'd said before failing miserably. "If God could forgive Peter and reach out to him, maybe there was a place for me as well." My pulse quickened at the indescribable way God quietly cultivated hope in a broken heart and the mystery in the knowing that he was near.

I wish I could write about thunderbolts and transformation but I can't. Instead it resembled Elijah hearing God's whisper.

In the midst of the commonplace and mundane, amidst the *everydayness* of this veiled rebirthing God saw me and met me. In the very ordinariness of slow days passing, the nugget of hope was revealed and began to glow brightly with unexpected life that would soon take my breath away.

Exposing Superman

He brought them out of darkness, the utter darkness, and broke away their chains.
Psalm 107:14

The heat was oppressive; my clothes were caked in dust and sweat. I sat in the shadow unable to recall when I'd last been free to do whatever I pleased. "What are you doing here?" A gentle voice asked - the hint of a smile in the tone.

I recognized the voice but I was silent.

Until that moment the past seven or eight years had rotated slowly around me, circling with pointed finger accusing, isolating, and derisively mocking. The words spat out from the darkness inside constantly maligning 'me'. Me failing, me falling, me struggling to claw my way back to a semblance of normality in a hostile world, alone. If only I'd been stronger, if I'd made better choices, if I'd trusted God, if I'd asked for help, if I'd not been so impatient, if I'd been a better husband, if.. if…if….

I never thought I'd hear his voice again…

I'd failed to appreciate the complexity, the breadth and depth of the battle, the relentless sadistic enemy I'd underestimated. He taunted me with a ventriloquist's dexterity constantly tossing negative words in my mouth. And like the frog in boiling water I never realized how distorted my perceptions and worldview had become. I'd placed myself at the center of my self-reliant world.

"There's no battle in the spiritual realm. It's a manner of speech," I flashed back to Oxford, to a lecture on philosophy of religion. The lecturer was in his mid-30's, white clerical band around his neck. "Whenever people can't explain something they fall back on God," he pronounced, pacing at the front of the class. "Philosophers call it the God of the gaps, but it's a lazy way of avoiding hard questions."

I shuddered at the arrogance that dismisses what it cannot explain and shuns the supernatural. It reduces Christianity to religion and stories, a collection of symbols, metaphors, folktales and ethics. It plucks out self-selected role models and guidelines for living a good life; and somewhere in the mix is a mystical, far-off God. These past seven years had given every opportunity for my head to take charge and figure out the meaning and path for my life without God. I saw no gaps. No sense of mystery. No hope.

"I cannot sustain this delusion," I cried as my spirit protested when my head dragged it back and forth across my angry landscape. The Oxford philosopher had no answers for my heart, and my rebellion had isolated and exposed me to a spiritual battle I could not explain.

I hardly comprehended. "Do you honestly believe satan is real?"

"Yes and no," I replied. I was just as self-assured as the irritating lecturer, basking in the glory of my degrees, my education, and my great ability to argue and debate. All crumbled to dust during long years of wandering desolation. And now as the scales fell from my eyes I was discovering how lost, how misguided, how imprisoned I'd become.

I was listening to some pastor on the Internet teaching about regaining freedom, that we live in a world of two realms where good and evil affect us for better or for worse. Jesus didn't walk this earth to generate Sunday school stories and endure an unfortunate accident; he was on a mission. God was not an optional extra depending for his existence on my agreement. Indignant as I might be at the thought, I had no say about participating in this conflict. Supernatural reality was no more dependent upon my acknowledgement or approval than was the law of gravity.

I assimilated old and new truths with relish, a beggar feverishly devouring chunks of bread that tasted fresh!

Until the day my epiphany exploded, flashing a vivid picture in my mind - a voice in my ear - and a rapid quickening of hope in my heart.

Long snaking leather whips snapped around me; knifing through the air. Drivers shouted from behind rhythmically goading slave gangs struggling to haul massive stones up ramps under a merciless sun. The dust of chiseled rock filled the air around me as I toiled, trapped in the same routine every day, for months, years. Identities were long gone; hope had perished, buried with the dead in the tombs of the rich they were building amidst the vast desert sands.

I huddled in the shadow of a half-built pyramid – exhausted, barely hanging onto survival. When into my spirit the voice whispered, "What are you doing here?"

I said nothing.

"Open your shirt," the invisible stranger said.

Reluctantly, I complied. Calloused fingers tore at the tattered garment until it parted to reveal a blazing Superman emblem beneath. I gasped through chapped lips – how did that get there?

"You've forgotten your identity, haven't you? Who you are; where you belong? *Remember* my son, now walk out of here."

The revelation flashing through my mind continued with startling clarity as I rose to my feet, *"Of course,* I thought. *How could I have been so stupid?"* Energy and power flooded through me; I was growing larger in stature. At the same time I heard my prison guards – a demonic presence I sensed around me, exclaim, *"Sh*t, he knows!"* as they withered to the ground, collapsing like deflated balloons. Courage and an unexpected rush of anger and confidence propelled me forward.

"Now walk into your freedom and trust *Me*," the voice said.

Throughout the experience the overwhelming sense I had was one of authority reawakened as if from a long nightmare. I walked out unafraid through the slaves and drivers who stepped back in fear as they caught sight of me and the emblem on my chest. And I repeatedly muttered to myself in amazement, "John, how could you get stuck here for so long?"

The image in my mind lasted less than a minute as I sat at my desk listening to the talk that had faded into the background. On the surface nothing changed, yet within me the world was in glorious turmoil. I may have looked like Clark Kent but now I knew I was Superman!

'Spiritual conflicts' often manifest in our lives as temptations, wrong choices, childhood abandonment, self-sufficiency, depression etc. Any one, or more, of those might have roots in our history and/or present circumstances. But below the surface an enemy camouflaged with seductive appeal infiltrates deep within and activates them. It's like walking into a radioactive zone; the fact that I see and feel nothing around me is irrelevant. Before long the effect of my exposure to radiation will manifest in my body. I felt as if I now had X-ray vision enabling me to see a dimension of reality I'd previously been oblivious to.

For years I lived in isolation, angry with God, feeling abandoned and betrayed. Working to make ends meet while groping through the dark never-ending maze of depression. I lived in bitterness, a slave whose master taunted with jibes and mocking laughter. "Told you not to trust Him. Look at you. He doesn't care. You could have been really successful. You're on your way now, aren't you?"

I forgot, I forgot, I forgot! God never changes. He has no favorites. He loves with more passion and adoration than any parent. He is not persuaded or manipulated by tantrums or sulking. I forgot so much in my anger and despair when my naïve ignorance years before allowed my eyes to be blindfolded and my spirit to be kidnapped.

A few days later this theme of forgetfulness resonated again as I watched the movie "Away from Her," the adaptation of an Alice Munro book.

Grant leaned in the doorway, watching the woman beside the tall man seated at a table across the room. She was quite oblivious to Grant's presence. Her hair was tied back; wisps tumbled in soft ringlets around her face reflecting silver gold in the warm morning light filtering through the window. A thick lump swelled in his throat as she smiled at the man seated beside her. She caressed his arm with unmistakable affection. Grant turned and shuffled down the hallway aching for the whisper and touch of his estranged wife.

Their marriage had gently undulated over fifty years. Yet the challenge of raising children had not come close to the trauma of these past five years. Fiona's diagnosis of Alzheimer's had finally broken wild and loose. With careless indifference more brain cells were snuffed out. Like blowing out candles on a birthday cake, one by one, slowly her light was reduced– allowing the vulture of black darkness to descend.

Many emotional conversations later they agreed that Fiona would take residence in this "place of care" when she could no longer cope and enjoy her independence. The move had broken Grant's heart. Her journey away from him was all the more painful when physically she was 'right there'. That was his reality to have and to hold while she melted before his eyes into a place he could not follow.

The story poignantly describes the loss of identity, understanding and companionship.

It caused me to wonder what would happen if the whole world were infected with Alzheimer's disease and every living creature helplessly transmitted it from one generation to the next. No one would have any memory that there once was a time when things were different.

I descended into just such a valley - where forgetfulness enfolds like a shroud. And I was lost in the mist of confusion obliterating the horizon.

With vision and memory blurred, I trailed along with the crowd traipsing through the world and wrongly concluding it to be my ultimate truth. "This is all there is to life," I'd murmured, "No reality but this. And I'm in sole control of my destiny." Mistrust spread like wildfire and jealousy absorbed my aspirations.

I fabricated a love affair with the world, insisting this upside down world was real. I was living in a prison camp, far from the purposes God originally intended.

Or maybe I forgot, because of how desperately I wanted not to remember. The lie became my truth and I bought it with conviction.

But the memory of the truth had planted deep within and refused to die though locked inside. In my heart of hearts I knew that Jesus was not the one responsible for my fall, but what to do about it? That was beyond my grasp at the time.

I pondered the many 'what if's' that barred me from gazing at the positive. Perhaps it was indeed God's Spirit leading my inner dialogue. "What if God is not responsible for your predicament? What if he genuinely wants to help you? What would it be like to begin to talk to God as if he were on your side saying 'yes' rather than your presuming it's always 'no John?' What if he truly does love you as a father loves a child? What if he grieves your struggle as much as the father lamented his prodigal son's decisions and actions that set them far apart from one another?"

That's when I heard a voice in my mind encouraging me to tear open my shirt! The Superman emblem was a reminder of who I really was – a deeply loved member of God's household taken prisoner by deception, parasites, and lies. I needed to be rescued, restored, and reaffirmed of my inheritance that carries all authority: on earth - as in heaven.

I shoved my chair back from the computer. My heart raced. A light had been flicked on and I could feel my spirit had a heartbeat once again. I went downstairs to grind fresh coffee, savoring the aroma. The kettle boiled and I chuckled as I poured.

"Superman drinks coffee, now what?"

Absolutely nothing had changed in my surroundings or circumstances. But strength was rising to overcome the vehement "No" that had taken up residence. And "Yes" moved in with conviction and a sigh of joy.

It would take me a while to fully comprehend the impact. But change had begun.

The long traverse through a troubled wasteland into the Promised Land would prove every bit as testing as the years in slavery. The difference was I now had a guide. And I had my identity. And a renewed sense of hope arose to provide direction.

I was being resurrected.

Hearing Again

He will cover you with his feathers, and under his wings you will find refuge; his faithfulness will be your shield and rampart. You will not fear the terror of night, nor the arrow that flies by day....
Psalm 91: 4-5

I'd returned to rain and snow in Canada in January, to my half-built house, an on-and-off relationship and my two cats. Money hemorrhaged out like water in the gutter with little flowing back to replenish the dwindling supply. I stared through the window trying desperately to sustain the sense of hope I'd fleetingly touched in England, to counter the swirling fog that mocked me for believing God cared.

What change could possibly be coming other than losing my house?

Clark Kent doesn't bear the slightest resemblance to Superman. Yet in the snap of a finger the transformation is complete from geek to hero. I hadn't yet grown into the Superman emblem, which I knew instinctively with the revelation symbolized how God sees me. The only clue about how to claim it was to believe in the promise, walk forward in faith, and trust. Quite how that would unfold, remained a mystery.

I was hungry to hear and know God as a relevant, living friend and power in my life after so many years of neglect, rebellion, and licking my wounds. But I had no idea how or what I was supposed to be listening to. In early years through university and ministry walking with Him meant a sense of perspective, being part of something greater than myself.

I remember being so inspired when attending conferences with John Wimber (founder of the Vineyard Church) as he encouraged us to believe that Jesus still heals today. At last here was someone who stepped down from the podium and modeled what he taught – God is alive and is here right now – doing today what Jesus did on earth 2,000 years ago. My heart leaped within me, burning with anticipation my spirit flooded with hope and passion.

Knowing and relying on God had given me direction and a strength within that I failed to find in my solitary wanderings beating my own path through life. Relationships fell far short, business was fickle, and people were frustrating – unable to provide the security and quality of an unconditional love that never failed.

I'd yet again reconnected with Catherine where we both contributed to our incessant rollercoaster ride while Karin had moved on and was now in a relationship, engaged. I also missed the community and camaraderie of a church family where I wasn't so isolated.

Like the prodigal son I was turning for home and not at all sure how to get there. It may have seemed small, but to me, the change was huge. On the brink of bankruptcy trying to stay afloat, I still teetered precariously on the cliff edge of ruin. I could take matters into my hands and try to get any job doing whatever came to hand. Or I could trust what I sensed God saying and take a leap of faith beyond that edge where I would have to give up my last sliver of control.

What happened next helped me jump… not into a suicide plunge, but into a calculated freedom from needing to know what would give Superman a mission. Invariably God's pathway ahead is revealed one step at a time, one day at a time – almost at the last minute.

His presence and purpose so often bursts from the most innocent seed that falls almost unnoticed into our lives. When it finally blossomed for me I knew it was no coincidence. The timing and perfection of it left little doubt that he was up to something. Nevertheless I was excited and apprehensive at the same time.

Having enjoyed Graham Cooke's writing, out of curiosity I googled his website and discovered that he was speaking at a conference less than an hour's drive from my house. It wouldn't have mattered what the topic was I recognized the tug of God's Spirit. I'd been so long in the wilderness, the relief of sensing God drawing closer- even if it seemed like a straw – was enough to make my heart jump..

I sighed with anticipation and prayed, "Okay, Lord, please humor me. If you want me to attend this conference, please confirm it in a way I can hear is really you."

Soon I'd come across a truth I love to repeat. God is able and willing to speak loud enough for us to hear. His ability to be heard is always greater than our deafness. If I desire to discern his voice he will ensure I hear it.

And God did confirm, in spectacular fashion. The people he used had no idea that he was speaking through them. Yet from my perspective as soon as they spoke I knew he was answering my request – and then some.

One Sunday afternoon a friend knocked on my door on his way home from a squash tournament. Rocking back in a chair by the fire (and not prompted by me) he said, "Do you know that Graham Cooke is speaking next month in Courtenay?" I smiled and relayed to him my story.

The following week, I traveled down-island to meet another friend for lunch at a country pub. I hadn't seen him for a while and we'd both endured challenging times. As I munched on my burger I tossed out the news that I was contemplating going to Graham Cooke's conference and asked. "Have you heard of him?"

"Of course!" he said. "We attended a conference a few years ago. It was so inspiring and refreshing. I'll come with you if you like!" His enthusiasm convinced me to tell my story again.

Once more, later that evening I returned home and checked my email. At the top was a note from my friend Simon on the other side of the world in London. "Johno, I thought you might be interested to know that Graham Cooke is speaking at a conference not far from where you live….." I smiled and replied with my story.

"Ok Lord, I hear you." I registered and committed myself to attend the following month wondering why it was so important. I wouldn't know the complete answer for another year.

Meanwhile I was doing piecemeal work for the contract we were winding down that required hardly more than one day per week of my time. How was I going to survive? I asked God what I was going to do. Fear interlaced with expectancy around a frayed thread of ever-present anxiety as I walked a tightrope between hope and despair from day to day. The slightest flicker of faith was growing in me to dare to believe God had me in the palm of his hand. And though his hand may have been steady as a rock, my palms were sweating.

I continued the renovation of my rustic cabin into a rustic house, completing two bedrooms and an en suite washroom. With meager resources I built, salvaged and restored every bit I could. Working on the washroom, I concluded that the elevated white basin I was about to install really didn't suit the space visually. Searching around I discovered a beautiful Italian marble basin at the tile shop but balked at the price, it was *so* right, but way beyond my shoestring budget!

I agonized for a day or two, and then decided the white basin just didn't cut it and held my breath as I foolishly purchased the perfect one I couldn't afford. What happened next I'd never experienced before in my life.

When I returned home, Italian marble basin in hand, a white envelope lay on the doormat at my front door. There was no note or identification – but $500 in cash was inside. The timing was exquisite. I was stunned, thrilled, and so moved.

"Lord," I said choking with emotion, "thank you so much… whoever this is… bless them!"

Then I heard God whisper. "This is for the basin; it really looks good doesn't it? I love what you're doing in that washroom. I want you to know that I'm generous and I love you – as a dad should… but much, much more than you can comprehend."

I was speechless; again I wanted to protest. It was too much. So extravagant it made me feel guilty. But his voice continued in my spirit, "John, don't worry about what lies ahead I'll take care of you…. You work on renovating your house and I'll work on renovating you. You're no longer a slave."

I stood on that doorstep clutching the envelope and a picture-story immediately played out in my mind. I saw two giant hands holding people by their ankles and gently shaking them as money tumbled from their pockets. "I have piggy banks all over the world," I heard, "And can release resources whenever I want to – trust me, keep walking, you'll see that I'm trustworthy." I wanted to interject again about needing to earn whatever was required but he insisted, "You are a dearly loved child, rest in me and trust me... what I'm teaching you cannot be earned – only received."

I felt bathed in acceptance, hope and love. I was no longer alone striving to make things happen. God was beginning to break through my wounded heart to reconfigure my lost identity. I sensed the slave clothes tearing away and exposing the 'Superman' emblem on my chest. And there in my work clothes, the expensive basin paid for in full, it felt every bit as miraculous as Moses parting the Red Sea.

The Superman emblem affirmed the truth that I was indeed a prodigal son of God my Father – not lost but found, never abandoned but forgiven. The beat of a drum pounded out a rhythm to the words, "Trust me and keep walking into freedom." I felt energized, yet utterly bemused about how it would all play out. Perhaps I was learning how to live from the inside out, where God's Spirit and my deeper identity were more real than my outward circumstances.

I thumbed through the Old Testament to the book of Joshua. God was preparing him as a leader to enter the Promised Land. Six or seven times he's admonished to be "strong and very courageous". God reiterates that he will be present with Joshua and his people and most importantly, "I will give you every place where you set your foot." I read the encouraging words as if they were for me as well: "Meditate on the Book of the Law every day.... Do not be terrified, do not be discouraged.... No-one will be able to stand against you."

In the days and months ahead I would return to those words many times as the journey unfolded according to a script I could never have imagined, let alone written.

"OK, I've got the picture, God," I said staring at the dreariest part of winter. But can you please hurry the process up a bit?"

In the movies, music plays and we fast forward through the mundane growth phase to the exciting and jaw-dropping climax. Why can't real life be more like the fantasy? The road into my future was a painfully slow journey; it often felt like tiptoeing on paper-thin ice that could give way at any time. I was still very alone and the threat of becoming insolvent hounded me like a hungry dog.

For much of the time my faith swung suspended between the paradoxes of fear and confident anticipation. What made the difference was a growing and inexplicable assurance that God was at work when I'd trust the process and believe *before* seeing. I encouraged myself with reading teaching resources I accessed on the internet. This hunger in itself was a remarkable change from previous years when I'd been totally unmotivated.

My enthusiasm ebbed and flowed; too well aware of how my self-esteem was measured by tangible signs of success and how hard it was to wait without feeling useless. Maybe I was deluding myself and needed to get a real job! How do I abide in God's love - the love of the Father – to the same degree that I hoped my daughters could trust me? Incarnating the intellectual idea of trust was the ever-present challenge.

When the day of the conference finally arrived, I wondered why it was so significant for me to attend. I had a vague sense of anticipation amidst a jumble of confusion and unanswered questions.

I walked across the parking lot and into the main entrance of the modern church complex and immediately bumped into Fred. I'd known him for years from the church I'd pastored in Port Alberni – the one I'd also betrayed and left in disgrace. He greeted me with a smile and a hug. I responded with a grunt and a sarcastic comment. I'd hoped to remain anonymous. He told me the whole leadership team was there, and to be honest, in that moment they were the very last people I wanted to see.

I sat at the back of the conference hall while the Port Alberni group clustered together on the left. Over the two days I chatted with most of them whom I'd known so well; each seemed genuinely delighted to see me in this context after so many years. One time I looked over and noted that all of them had been on my leadership team ten years earlier. Where are the new people? "It's not all wasted, John," I heard the Lord say.

Yet mostly, I felt the constant need to be affirmed and validated conflicting with the nagging sense of deep injustice I couldn't shrug off.

Graham Cooke spoke of his struggle and that when he rebelled against God he seemed "even more 'blessed". The relentless kindness of the Lord wooed him back.

"Good for you," I muttered. "I've felt cursed and abandoned with obstacle after obstacle, year after year." I was really beginning to get irritated.

I knew from his books he was a man of integrity who'd weathered some severe storms. He synthesized the radical reality of God creatively and authentically and backed it up with a gifted prophetic ministry and a lifestyle of faith with a servant heart. After his talk I approached the podium and mentioned my response and my struggle. He listened and we prayed together for my years under "the curse of Job" to come to an end.

A few of the Alberni group asked if I was intending to "return to ministry". I was non-committal. I didn't have a clue how that would possibly happen. Someone encouraged me saying how great it would be, but I couldn't receive it. All I could feel was a familiar anger rising. *Yes I'm sure it is,* I thought. *But how the hell am I going to make ends meet?* They had no idea how desperate I felt inside... and how alone.

At the end of the conference Graham invited pastors to stand to receive prayer, and I surprised myself by rising to my feet. My eyes were closed as he spoke over us. Those who were there said he pointed straight at me and pronounced that all that had been lost would be restored. I didn't know that detail until years later even though they went home excited on my behalf.

As the conference ended I went up to the pastor who was leading my old church. I offered him my hand, "Bill, if there's anything I can do to support you please let me know... it's been a long road." He shook my hand and said 'thank you', but I could read his eyes. He'd never consider such an offer. I'd fallen. I would never be forgiven, or at least never be allowed back in.

For the first time something like spiritual recovery appeared to be possible, but how? It was crazy? Who would take me and how would I get there?

I had no endowment or family support. It would have to be the road travelled by the walking wounded – the slower one-day-at-a-time way. I knew from Biblical characters that God was quite capable and willing to restore and use a broken life guilty of horrendous crimes. Moses murdered in anger, David murdered and committed adultery,

Gideon was a coward, Saul killed Christians, Peter denied Jesus, and the list goes on.

I felt like Lazarus shuffling out of the grave as the sound of Jesus' voice called him back to life. The grave clothes still had to be removed but a massive stone of death and unbelief had been rolled away and with the breath of life came hope. And that hope was in knowing that if God still had time for me after all that had transpired then maybe I had a future with him after all. That was more important to me than the approval of any human being.

"Suppose we'll wait and see how this works out from here," I mused, picking up the tools the next day to continue the piecemeal work on my long renovation project.

Help My Unbelief

With tears flowing, the child's father at once cried out, "I do believe! Help my unbelief!"
Mark 9:24

Most of my life I believed in God – but was ambivalent about his power to do anything immediate or tangible. I had little confidence or certainty that he would provide for me financially if I dared risk saying yes to him again; I mean caring for basic needs, not releasing vast wealth.

I'll never forget the day I stared over another precipice, this time pending bankruptcy. It was Friday around 2 pm when I learned that any prospect of cashing in a life insurance policy was not going to work. It was my last possible source of income apart from selling my car and house.

I had no job, no prospects. With barely $300 in the bank and the cupboards almost bare. I blankly stared at an empty computer screen - at a loss to know what to do or where to begin.

It seemed the weight of the world pressed down across my shoulders like a heavy yoke and my fleeting optimism was crushed by circumstances I didn't know how to control. Despair rose like a dark breaking wave.

"What now?" In desperation I cried out to God. "I'm saying *yes* to your call on my life. If you want my house and my car you can have them – I'm holding nothing back, and I'm scared…. where else is there for me to go?" I trailed off in a whisper.

I'd arranged to meet friends for dinner that night but didn't want to go. I knew I'd be asked about my situation and I was weary of my pathetic story, always struggling, constantly in need. If there's one thing worse than being in a place of dark desperation, it's being continually humiliated by reminders of your inability to get out on your own. It had been seven years! Nothing had resolved. My relationships were still a mess, business ventures had crashed and burned, and I had nothing left to say.

A few years earlier I'd lent a friend some money to save his business and the promise to repay me had not materialized. It was a large sum I never saw again. Financially, no matter what I attempted, nothing worked. While God's promise for provision was deeply encouraging, I always felt like a kid trying to justify asking for pocket money.

I went for dinner. And when the inevitable question came, "How are things going John?" I answered as truthfully as I could.

"I knew you'd ask me. I'm probably more tired of my depressing answers than you are." Nonetheless I recounted portions of my trip to England, the fading business prospects and the more encouraging story of finding $500 on my doorstep. I shared my growing sense of God nudging me back into ministry. I described the recent conference and the strange sense of possible restoration awakening within me that had taken me by surprise.

Deon listened intently, "What do you think you'll need to make it through in a month?" she asked leaning forward. I responded with a figure that was a bare minimum.

"Come on John," Blake interjected, "It can't be as bad as that. I always knew ministry was your first calling and you should return to it."

"Easy for you to say, I know where I'm meant to be heading; the question is how?" I shook my head as I munched another mouthful of the meal they were paying for.

Deon smiled, "There are many people who care about you John. Maybe we can get in touch with some of them and see what we can do."

"Thank you so much," I replied with a lump in my throat. "It's embarrassing to be in this situation – it's been so long."

I drove home in tears…. The rain fell on roads glistening wet black, arching and turning in the reflected orange glow of lamp posts like the back of a great killer whale. I was glad I'd ventured out. A faint glimmer of hope flickered and I felt more supported and loved than I had in a long, long time.

Maybe the miracle could happen after all. Friendship and small acts of kindness could overcome the looming assassin of loneliness.

The next day, I was painting the recently completed master bedroom upstairs when there was an unexpected knock on the door. The folk music station from Wales was blaring as Fred and Glenda appeared downstairs to invite me out for supper. I showed them what I'd accomplished around the house and agreed to meet them, glad for the company.

On his way out the door Fred drew a roll of $650 from his pocket. "This is for you to go to another conference next week with Graham Cooke. We collected the money this morning when the men got together for breakfast. There are many people who love you John, and still believe in you," he said patting me on the shoulder, lips quivering as he fought back tears.

I was speechless. "Thank you," I turned to hide the emotion welling up in response to such unexpected generosity. Unless you've lived years of wandering alone, desperately trying to survive, weathered dark nights of sheer despair about the future, you can't imagine what it feels like to be so found, so supported, so rescued, so unexpectedly.

That evening I'd barely sat down in the restaurant when Fred announced that the same group of men had collected monthly pledges for me to receive a lump sum every month for the next 12 months to help support me during my return to ministry – whatever that would mean. Again, I was without words, in tears. So relieved and thankful, wondering where this was leading. I felt a new excitement. If God was working this out behind the scenes, if this was really him, then perhaps there was a future for me after all.

A few days later Fred called. "Just want you to know that the money will be deposited into your account on the 20th of each month; we've almost reached the target to provide a monthly base for the next 12 months," he declared with his trademark chuckle.

I thought I'd left ministry forever. I'd failed. I never wanted to be in the goldfish bowl of public scrutiny or risk such humiliation again. Now God was drawing me gently back through the very people I'd walked away from. I was humbled and moved when these men insisted on reminding me of my words spoken over ten years ago, 'You'd do the same for us."

I thanked the Lord that these desperately barren years were coming to an end. I knew in my spirit good things lay ahead. The relief of company on the journey, support restored and my solitary existence coming to an end was indescribable. I was apprehensive and must confess I wondered if it would last, but in my heart I knew this was for real. The wilderness was not a place to wander alone. From now on I intended to take every opportunity that came my way.

A week later, Seattle was in a torrential downpour that continued unrelenting until Washington was far behind us and daylight fading. Andrew and I drove through Oregon and Northern California heading south for the conference. Snow was falling in the mountains and we were fortunate to tailgate a snow plow over the pass as we continued through the night toward Vacaville; north of San Francisco.

I was eager to hear God and know him intimately again. I definitely had a healthy sense of the fear of him unlike I'd ever experienced before. It wasn't a negative fear, but a realization that things were changing. The train of God's plan was leaving the station and I wanted to make quite sure I was *on it*.

Being at the conference with a friend was refreshing and nurturing to my spirit - that dry place had shriveled into a prune years before. I could almost feel it absorbing the resurrected life and a new-found hope as I listened to the words from the stage. The message of trusting in the faithfulness of God fell on freshly fertile ground.

"Don't pray as a widow," Cooke exhorted. "Pray as God's bride! I recall his words so clearly to this day. "The wilderness is a place of testing, an opportunity to draw near to the heart of God – the Father. We are in the wilderness either by default or design. Learn to enjoy those places where you are taught to have faith in the Father despite feelings and circumstances."

Before heading home we decided to stay for the Sunday service. Andrew insisted that I be prayed over by some of the prophetic team who were students at a school the church hosted. I used to be afraid of what God may reveal but I wanted to trust him; to trust that his heart is always to inspire and never to humiliate or shame anyone. I sought to believe and embrace the prophetic, a gift exercised to encourage us to receive the love of the Father and to step into the purposes he has for us.

A group of five, who'd never met me before, spoke over me.

"You are very kind, and have a ministry of encouragement – you are wise and have a gift of teaching."

"I see a picture of strands woven together into a thick rope – outside…. working with young people; actively teaching about life skills," another shared.

"I have a picture of you walking out of a burned and charred landscape along a path that will be new but not unfamiliar. You're emerging from a cold damp cave – something like the one Elijah hid in. Don't try and do stuff. Allow the Lord to accomplish what he wishes in his time. You don't have to struggle to do anything – he will do it."

Then a gentle voice said, "God just wants you to know that he sees you as his friend and wants to reassure you that all these years have not been wasted."

Andrew and I drove back to Vancouver through the night. The roads were quiet and the skies dark with lots of time to think and listen.

"Trust me," I heard in my spirit. "Keep walking. Don't be afraid. Be strong and courageous."

"Jesus, thank you for being with me," I replied. "This is terrifying; such a slow process."

"Let's stop here for coffee," Andrew interrupted, pulling off the highway into the neon glare of a Chevron gas station. It was chilly in the night air; feather light flakes of snow gusted into the light from a dark and heavy sky. I offered to drive and before long we were back on the I-5 heading north.

"Only a few weeks ago I had no idea where I was going or what I'd be doing," I mused as I clutched the steering wheel. "Now I have this sense of a future, and that God's not finished with me." Like a jeweler stringing beads I laced together the events of the past months: my trip to England, visits and affirmations from family and friends, meeting leaders at the first conference, the financial support promised, and the words spoken over me earlier in the day by strangers.

"It can't all be meaningless coincidence," I assured my doubting heart. It skipped a beat in excited response. Hope and a quiet sense of anticipation filled the car. Andrew slept. But he wasn't the only one with me that night; I felt God's presence as a warm comforting peace.

"Everything's going to work out just fine, trust me."

"Trust me keep walking," resonated in my spirit like the 'clickety-clack' of a train riding the rails with a soothing metallic rhythm.

I wanted to believe but unbelief still threatened to derail me –and it very nearly did.

Persevering

He lifted me out of the slimy pit, out of the mud and mire; He set my feet on a rock and gave me a firm place to stand, He put a new song in my mouth, a hymn of praise to our God.
Psalm 40: 2-3

And then you're back at home and everything's the same.

No crowds, music or inspiring voices. Doubt seeps through the wounded cracks and challenges the fragile hope barely birthed. I had no idea what to do except believe for what I did not yet see and be patient. The provision of financial assistance over the next 12 months was an enormous infusion of confidence and trust. My heart brimmed with gratitude and relief, so appreciative of the kindness of those who'd contributed; humbled by their belief in me – when I'd virtually given up on myself.

Yet, my journey of restoration was no smooth ride. My emotions could still plummet frequently and some days I felt as though I was strapped into a rollercoaster. My weeks could have me travelling multiple roller-coasters. There were days when I struggled to believe that God was actually working or cared at all. Financial provision did not make it simple to 'live by faith,' providing little sense of direction or insight into what the future held. I could all too easily look back on the train wrecks of the past eight years and see disappointment and failure, the near-countless let-downs and isolation that had become my norm.

In the months following the conference in California I often cried out to God for encouragement.

I read books on faith and discovered a tenacity rising in me that determined to no longer entertain the negative as my truth. Amidst my struggle I was learning to trust and to dig deeper into abiding in the love of God the Father; something I continue to find a challenge – it ebbs and flows. I picked up my guitar and sang songs affirming the goodness of God and his faithfulness. Many times as I declared the words I sensed discouragement lift and a quiet assurance replace it. Perhaps if I'd lived in a bigger center I'd have attended a church but at this stage I still journeyed alone.

Every Wednesday I'd drive into Port Alberni to visit my daughters. I established a routine of joining friends at the pub beforehand; most of whom had become as disillusioned with church as I had – having also experienced arrogant or abusive leadership. One week after our usual banter over pints I was surprised when a friend I'd known for many years stood up and shook my hand.

"Hey bro' good to have you back, this is for you."

Within the handshake was a cheque. I thanked him with a hug but didn't unfold the paper until I got to my car. It was $1000, a significant contribution for another month's expenses. The spontaneous generosity caused tears to well up again and encouraged me that despite my ongoing battle to believe, God would indeed be faithful to provide. Faith only grows by risking steps into the unknown based on God's promises and goodness. Life experience cements that truth into our hearts, transforming concept into actual conviction releasing testimonies from our lips, "It is true, he does provide!"

God also speaks in the most unexpected circumstances to answer those shivering questions of trepidation and uncertainty. It happened a few weeks later at a social gathering with friends in Port Alberni. I was chatting with a few people when my younger daughter came into the room and stood by my side... I automatically embraced her... it's one of the most precious places/postures I know on earth. "That's how I feel about you," the Lord nudged.... "Abide in my embrace. Only there will you be enabled to share my love with others. Simply give away what you're receiving; it has to be fresh, like fish, today's catch."

As my assurance and understanding slowly grew I began to consider the unthinkable. Should I get in touch with some former members of the Anglican Church in Canada? I'd heard that others had been forced to leave buildings and venture out on their own after voicing similar concerns we'd expressed ten years earlier. This group had formed a Coalition, joining with others in the United States to forge a new path forward together.

I was clear in my heart that God was calling me back into ministry; I just didn't know how that would unfold. "No harm in pulling on a thread," I told myself as I apprehensively made my first effort to restore the relationship of mutual betrayal that had haunted me for so long.

I phoned one of the leaders of what I later discovered was a wounded group of churches smarting from the injustices meted out by the Canadian Church. He remembered me as the prophetic pioneer who crashed and burned and we agreed to meet for lunch. I said I was far from ready to actually do anything but was interested in "kicking the tires" of this new group.

I wondered whether there would even be a welcoming reception given the fact that I'd 'fallen'. I felt more like a returning prisoner of war who had been captured in the heat of battle and survived many years of isolation. I learned that no such understanding exists in much of Christianity. You're either in or you're out, and if you're out there are no extenuating circumstances – you're responsible, you make choices, and you're alone.

I was greeted warmly but with real caution as to whether I was 'healed and together' or still damaged goods. It seemed ironic to me that a Church with such an impaired track record should be somewhat surprised when the same caution was reciprocated. "I'm not sure I want to risk getting involved with the Anglican Church again," I admitted. "I know it may come across as arrogant, but I'm not really asking you for permission to do ministry. God has already convicted me of his grace and forgiveness. I just think it's good to belong somewhere, and seeing this is part of my DNA I thought I'd check it out."

A few months later I met again with some of the Canadian leaders who worked closely with the larger organization of disenfranchised Episcopal Churches in the United States known as the Anglican Mission. The leadership requested I write my story, and I did so, confessing my struggles and indiscretions. They requested four pages and I delivered fourteen.

I experienced a bizarre peace (beyond understanding perhaps) within me because I knew that God had already forgiven and accepted me. I also understood the need for integrity and full disclosure as part of my restoration and ongoing accountability. We agreed that I was not ready for leadership but would remain in relationship and see how the future unfolded. I appreciated the open door. Later I learned that some of the leaders wanted nothing to do with me.

I bristled at the reception; like a leper undergoing inspection, then told to return in six months, and "we'll see how you're doing." Nobody, it seemed was truly interested in who I was, what had happened, or what I'd learned. As so often happens in church, I felt pushed away rather than drawn closer.

I empathized with the woman caught in adultery, dragged into the marketplace before Jesus and accused by the religious leaders. I was a prisoner who had forgotten the Superman emblem on my chest. This was a spiritual battle. I could not relate to a formal institution or love an abstract concept of God. I'd walked for years with a sense of powerlessness, believing the deception that God had abandoned me - or at very least he seemed impotent in my life and indifferent to my circumstances.

I'd fallen to the brink of suicide and lost almost everything along the way. My life was not a concept and neither were my circumstances abstract theological principles. Over these years I'd become more aware than ever that I was not the center of the universe but caught up in a physical/spiritual realm much larger and more dynamic than I'd ever imagined or considered. Reduced to its essence I'd come face to face with good and evil as spiritual realities with power to either imprison me or release me.

The fulfilment and purpose we long for are intangible, spiritual qualities; love, joy, peace, patience, kindness, self-control, contentment, forgiveness, hope. The battle rages around *how* we attain them. Evil seduces with promises of power and success; feeding these insatiable yearnings through our physical senses. It offers wealth, travel, sex, drugs, career advancement, success, popularity, and suchlike – all dependent upon external resources. Good focuses within, placing God at our spiritual center and relationship with him as the source.

I experienced evil and succumbed, so when I finally said 'yes' to God again, it was no surprise I would be tested. The first targeted my identity and the second told me lies: 'Nothing really happened', 'the depression isn't gone', 'God isn't trustworthy – look what's happening around you'.

In those moments I resolved to declare God's promises over my cartwheeling emotions. I read psalms, listened to talks on the Internet, and wrote and sang songs affirming truths I believed in. When I sang alone in my room facing the wall... something shifted in my spirit. Light prevailed. It was grueling at times... but it worked.

Depression and religion resemble the estranged brother and sister of a family we dread to visit and pray won't come knocking on our door for a surprise sleepover. They carry with them an aura of heaviness, a passive resignation to the hardships of life, or the distant unknowable otherness of a cold God distilled into rules, superstition and ritual. Both disengage the human spirit and emotions. Depression withdraws and religion withholds.

I'd experienced depression for years but the religious bondage came into sharp focus when I was at the back of a church observing people attending a funeral. Most wore suits and were obviously 'on their best behavior'; there was a dignified formality throughout the procedure. I wondered how those present pictured God. Their demeanor suggested he was very serious, distant, impersonal, even frightening; someone to dress up for and make sure you don't offend. It was awful, despite the fact it was a somber occasion.

The contrast in behavior at the reception following couldn't have been more defined. People had cast their jackets aside; they were chatting and laughing in an atmosphere of relaxation and friendship. The emotion suppressed in the 'service' was much freer flowing in the conversations afterwards.

If my daughters acted nervous in my presence, read from a written script, and always wore their smartest clothes when visiting I would wonder what on earth was wrong with them. When talking to God, picture the scene where guests have left the house and the family remains. They're gathered around the fire; shoes are off, hair ruffled, perhaps a glass of wine in the hand; totally unwound, chatting and laughing together. Rather than kicking us out because we're disrespectful he's delighted that we're all together – communicating with head, heart, and body.

But in my long journey home I wasn't by the fireside yet. I was rediscovering the character of a Father God whose voice I'd heard and in whose presence I was beginning to feel as an inner hope and expectancy encouraging me to continue moving forward.

Transformation takes time. And I wanted to get to the destination. But God is no more willing to short circuit growth than a parent is prepared to have their child skip a few grades in order to graduate.

During this excruciatingly slow process I sang songs affirming God's faithfulness; believing in my spirit what I didn't yet see, singing with my head the truth I believed, and eventually receiving in my heart the power of the promises. The two core themes were my identity in relationship to God as a much-loved son, and faith to entrust him with my uncontrollable circumstances that looked like huge waves about to crash over me.

Ten years earlier I'd written a song about God being a safe place for me. It was strange opening up the file that I retrieved from my bookcase and re-reading the words I'd nearly destroyed and burned when all appeared lost.

You O Lord are a safe place to be
You O Lord are a safe place for me
You calm my heart
And you take all my fear
You draw me near with your love
You draw me near

You O Lord are a safe place to be
You O Lord are a safe place for me
Like a mighty river
From your heart to mine
Let your Spirit flow
In your love let it flow…

I was being drawn deeper into experientially knowing God as my Father who loved and accepted me unconditionally. I'd had fleeting sips that seldom lingered; but this was different. I'd never experienced this intimacy before. The concept in my head was sinking into my heart, and when that happens power is released. I wrote a chorus and the song was complete…

That you should be my Father
And I should be your child
Beloved by your side

In mercy reconciled
It's a wonder, it's a glory
It's a joy to be told
Abiding in your love… in the fullness of your love

Every day for two weeks I sang the words of the chorus….. and each time I couldn't make it through without tears running down my face. It was as if I was being picked up and held close to my father's heart. I experienced His presence with me. For the past seven years my strongest 'feeling' had been despair and a sense of resignation to struggle alone. The miracle within was a tender metamorphosis, where that deep loneliness was being replaced with the quiet affirmation that God was not finished with me yet.

I returned again and again. It felt so healing to experience a different emotion – that of being cared for. God's nurturing love saturated the dry sponge and soaked me from the inside out. This was legitimate love, healing love, liberating love in its purest form.

As I was worrying about possibly losing the house, or how enough money would come, or where my future employment might be I voiced my concerns to God while declaring my faith.

My life didn't magically change. I continued to pursue a relationship with Catherine thinking that we would soon be married. So much had been invested over the years; if God could forgive David and Bathsheba surely this relationship was not beyond redemption? Both our spouses had remarried but peace and confidence between us remained elusive. While I insisted there was a future Catherine was much more hesitant. She was perhaps more spiritually sensitive to the reality I didn't want to acknowledge, that God was not going to permit what had been illegitimately conceived to continue indefinitely. I argued that such a negative mindset left no room for God's grace, "People have done far worse and moved on."

Financially I lived on the edge and spent many days working on the house. Almost every day God encouraged me, "Keep walking, work on the house and I'll work on you, trust me."

I learned it was far more effective if the words in my head were declared aloud. When I sang of God's promises faith rose up and drowned out the fear and familiar negative discouragement. I began to see aspects of my journey in a new light as I referred back to the Exodus story and identified with the slaves being set free. How does one walk into the unbelievable – where you've never set foot or even dared to consider traveling? Once the slave is out of Egypt how does he exorcise Egypt?

I reflected on the familiar story of the Exodus after the Passover and tried to place myself within the context of that first morning after the angel of death had passed over the land. When sleepy eyes peered out of doorways, lintels caked with the dried blood of sacrificed lambs. The street was unchanged from yesterday and the house was no different. The occupants still lived in Egypt, the neighbor's dog barked too early and the rooster crowed too loudly. Breakfast had to be cooked over a fire that required tending; kids needed washing and food in their stomachs. Everything was exactly the same as the dawning of every other day, except everything was completely different.

Yesterday I would've looked out of the door as a slave but today it would take time to sink in. I was no longer a slave, I was free. Free to move from this place and enter into a new future – the Promised Land. God had won me my freedom, now I had to believe, receive, walk into it and possess it. Embracing my true identity was as challenging for me as I imagined it was for those slaves to live free. God didn't lead them into freedom alone and neither was he abandoning me.

When I first picked up my guitar and fingered chords never forgotten it was a lazy return to a well-worn path I'd avoided for years. Now, instead of evoking memories of what had been lost, anger, betrayal, and hurt at my predicament - I found to my delight that it was calling me forward toward a much brighter horizon. Lazy, because I revisited the familiar songs that I didn't have to learn. I'd once thought I'd never sing them again and now, behold, they were rising to the surface and touching my spirit.

God the Father knows his children and communicates in ways that connect with who we uniquely are. The years rolled back and the little boy who sang in the choir discovered his voice again. It was a gradual revelation. Seven years earlier the music stopped altogether and in my despair the inside was empty, a garbage dump of refuse. All I could do was recycle the darkness into poetic words describing the emptiness – there was no music, no melody line, no tune.

But now words came from heaven with melodious sounds. As I sang and wrote and cried light pierced the darkness and a garden began to grow amidst the wasteland and refuse. Singing was like gardening, releasing a sense of hope and anticipation even though external circumstances and personal challenges were slow to change. "Keep walking, trust me, work on the house and I'll work on you."

I was becoming more intentional about feeding my spirit, like an athlete who's been injured returns to physiotherapy in the gym to rebuild his damaged body and weak muscles. I read the gospel account of Jesus as he established relationships with men and women who were constantly amazed and confused by his supernatural acts of kindness and compassion. I walked through the beginnings of the early church as described in Acts and wanted the same sense of wonder and power of God's presence to be my experience.

My friend Simon put me in touch with another prophetic man in London who had great sensitivity and gifting. I hesitatingly recounted some of my awkward story and fall from grace. Instead of silence he encouraged me with transparent testimony of how God had rescued and restored him. Company was joining me on this journey.

Strength rose within me as the shell of a man shuffled out of the grave like Lazarus waking from the dead.

"Hi John, would you be interested in doing some research from home to help us prepare for our World Leadership and Management Conference?"

My heart jumped as I chatted with Simon. It was May and the call from Germany surprised me more than the cell phone vibrating on my hip. Simon was the World Vice President of Human Resources for a well-known airline company. He explained the opportunity as I clutched the phone to my ear and paced the pavement at the top of the driveway in the spring sunshine. "Would you be ok if we paid normal consulting rates?" he asked. *Acceptable?* I told him it would be extremely generous and I did my best to remain calm and not scream, "Yes!"

I had no problem taking hold of any work opportunity that came my way and wasn't interested in trying to write a script about how the future would unfold. I heard the whisper of God again, "I told you I'd take care of you."

During my visit to England over Christmas I'd so nearly not spent a day with Simon in London because of my anger from past disappointments. At times of deep struggle one is hyper-sensitive and undoubtedly places unreasonable expectations on others. So when I'd communicated my dark valley to a few close friends years before it had come as a shock when my forlorn cry for help was met with silence. I'd harbored anger since then and could easily have justified not responding to Simon earlier in the year. The result would have been an ongoing disconnect in our friendship.

Before Simon hung up I'd accepted his invitation. I didn't have to pray about this one. The sun seemed warmer and brighter; my heart beat faster as I wondered how many significant events, and life-changing possibilities, swing like hinges on what I could easily disregard as insignificant opportunities?

The next six weeks were the most enjoyable and fulfilling I'd had in eight years. I busied myself with research for a business management exercise and traveled twice to Frankfurt for conferences. The second was to participate in the company's smaller international leaders' gathering where I presented and facilitated a workshop on personality styles that I'd used in consulting. I stayed in a first class family hotel across the road from the Black Forest, had time to catch up with Simon, visited Heidelberg and reconnected with a friend in Zurich. I felt I was touching the hem of true Life and Hope; totally sure that this was God's timing and provision.

The opportunities were stimulating and affirming while generating a healthy injection of cash into my account that significantly helped with costs for the rest of the year. Though it didn't continue long, it was confidence-building and exciting to imagine and dream.

My routine returned to a more familiar pattern and I was back to singing those songs again and working to apply faith and hope to my uncertain future. However I was learning that *process* is God's preferred method of training and *patience* is a vital paving stone in the pathway forward. It had been six months since I'd visited England and attended my first conference and there had been extended pauses in-between bursts of activity and opportunity. But those 'bursts' were to assure me that God's hand was upon me. I was encouraged to believe that this walk of trust (you build the house while I build you) was underway – maybe more that I realized.

With every passing day the same message repeated with quiet affirmation, "Keep walking and trust me. You are my son whom I love and I'm pleased with you." I was to keep the Superman emblem clearly visible, take hold of my true identity as a son set free from slavery, and walk in authority (which meant challenge negativity with God's promises).

Step by step God my Father was showing me that He meant what He said; "All I have is yours". Confidence poured into my parched spirit releasing strength, peace, hope, and a sense of anticipation I had no desire to resist. Life welled up like a fountain I couldn't turn off.

And the change was undeniable. The revelation of who I was in God's hands broke the stranglehold of the curse over my slave/orphan heart. I believe the core of depression is love lost and identity confused. Internal loss and bitterness expands to engulf you, all appreciation of oneself evaporates with everything else positive in life. One loses control, surrendering authority and initiative to 'fate'; never daring to hope or dream – there's no energy for such unimaginable foolishness. The invisible prison of circumstances becomes our taskmaster, and we are rendered powerless victims. I camped for years in that destitute ghetto aware I desperately needed liberation and yet was unable to do anything about it.

Fortunately even the half-hearted whisper for help is enough for God. I found Jesus staring me in the face with that divine quizzical smile speaking love, acceptance, and complete knowing without one word uttered. He placed an arm across my shoulders, turned me around and showed me the path ahead. The revelation was; for freedom and a future to materialize I merely had to choose to step forward – with him.

Jesus entered this troubled earth and lived without succumbing to despair or depression. His example melted me once again to a posture of trust. As God's love in human form, he reestablished my identity as His beloved, and my healing accelerated with bewildering grace.

In time, I sensed my life was becoming an amazing and unexpected story.

News of a friend's death broke out of the blue with shocking suddenness. I knew his family well and amongst the crowd of friends at his funeral I couldn't help but share some memories from the open mike. It was the first time I'd spoken in a church for eight years, and people approached me afterwards to say how good it was to hear me speak. "You have such a gift; you captured Jeff so well." The words were encouraging but inside I panicked. The thought of returning to where I'd shattered into a million pieces was terrifying.

There was more to come; unpredictable was beginning to feel normal.

An Unexpected Crisis

Then they cried to the Lord in their trouble, and he saved them from their distress. He sent out his word and healed them; he rescued them from the grave.
Psalm107: 19-20

It was a warm sunny afternoon; blue sky.

Perfect for working outside putting the finishing touches to my deck. I was on my knees carefully applying a protective sealant over the cedar boards when the phone rang. At first I didn't recognize the voice on the other end but from the sound of it, it wasn't good news. I stood up and placed the paintbrush on the tin after replacing the lid.

"What happened?" I asked.

"Apparently Karin collapsed at the gym a short while ago," her fiancé Rob said, his voice surprisingly calm. "The surgeon says it's not looking good right now. She had multiple seizures. They'll be airlifting her to Victoria in a few hours." A thousand thoughts rushed through my mind as I absorbed the news. "I'm so sorry Rob. Have the girls been told yet?"

He sighed, "No, I thought it best to call you first."

"Thanks. I appreciate that. I'll get hold of Michelle and we'll meet you there."

How quickly things change. I called the hospital and spoke to the surgeon I knew. Karin had suffered an aneurism but his tone and words indicated a high probability she wouldn't survive. I called Michelle who was spending a few days with friends and told her the news as sensitively as I could with a lump in my throat.

"Is she going to die?" she asked through a flood of tears.

"I don't know, my dear, the doctor says it doesn't look good."

We arranged to meet and headed down to the hospital in Victoria. My other daughter was within a week of returning to Canada from London and I decided to wait until we had more information before contacting her.

It was well after 9 pm as we trekked to Victoria, our conversation full of questions, and empty of answers. I tried to offer hope while preparing Michelle for the very real prospect of losing her mother. Arriving at the hospital we headed up to the emergency unit and shortly thereafter the helicopter crew appeared wheeling Karin down the hallway.

Rob joined us and we chatted while we waited. Eventually we were escorted to Karin's room where she lay unconscious amidst drips and tubes. Rob remained outside contacting her parents. I'd known them for years but times had changed.

Michelle stood at one side of the bed crying and stroking Karin's hair. I gently placed my hand on her forehead and prayed with Michelle for God to release his healing into her. I declared God's goodness and the authority he's given us for healing power to overcome the curse of sickness and evil. That was all we could do – but it was so much more than I'd have been able to declare even six months earlier.

The life we'd shared for so many years earlier came flooding back. My betrayal and the pain I caused, our inability to connect, and how estranged we'd become. Now here we were. I was praying for a miracle for Karin's healing and if she recovered she'd probably be oblivious to the emotional traumas of this strange night.

After more consultations and assessments Karin seemed to stabilize and I decided to drive back up island while Michelle stayed with a friend to remain close by. We'd agreed that it would be wise for me to contact my older daughter Carmen and arrange an early flight home as we didn't know what the future held. It was a relief to get behind the wheel. The streets were tranquil as I drove the winding route home. I reflected about our life together and the ripping end to our marriage – the wounds were very tender that night.

At home, sleep was elusive and after a few hours, I called Carmen in London. Fortunately she was spending the last week with a close friend whom she'd known since childhood. She answered brightly.

"Oh hi, Dad. Fancy you calling. What's up?"

"Where are you?" I asked.

"Well actually, you won't believe this but I'm in a cab with Sarah heading for the police station. I've just had my passport stolen."

I couldn't believe it. I commiserated with her and said I'd call back in a few hours. Meanwhile I contacted the Canadian authorities to gain temporary identity documents for her as soon as possible.

When we talked again, she crumpled on the sidewalk in tears. A policeman helped her and friends and family in England rallied to have her on a flight home the next day.

Rob offered his house and was very hospitable and composed during a time that must have been excruciating for him as well.

When Karin's brother called, I broke down, exhausted, revisiting the grief of our broken marriage while attempting to comfort two frightened daughters. We'd hardly begun to talk when the tears gushed out of me. It caught Ken by surprise.

When it happened again as I spoke to Fred a few hours later I realized how much unfinished business was still locked up inside. Perhaps it was another level of emotional release and healing that was processed.

The next day Carmen arrived surprisingly poised. "I had no more tears left," she reflected later. When we visited Karin she was beginning to wake up without any recollection of what had happened since visiting the gym. The next ten days were delicate including an eight hour brain operation to cauterize the aneurism. Prayers for her recovery were answered and all ended well. But in that experience I couldn't ignore the irony.

No-one questions aneurisms, the trauma, and the impact of bleeding on the brain, a sudden collapse, and medical teams responding to the distress. Yet while depression and emotional meltdown is a much more insidious and widespread disease, and at least equally devastating to family and friends, it's harder to diagnose and treat. Most sufferers are never airlifted out by any team to get them going again.

Shortly after Karin returned home, I drove up to the house to visit the girls. She was watering the garden; the setting sun ignited the stream of water flowing from the hose and cast a glow over her face and hair. I was struck by a new peace and tranquility that seemed to rest upon her. In that poignant moment I caught a fleeting glimpse of the love we had lost; lovers now become strangers, one flesh torn apart. And I mourned the loss of our family.

No matter what else happens after the marriage vows are broken, somehow there's an emotional tie that is never entirely severed. Later on, during the occasional birthday dinner or holiday meal, you may glance over when the other is unaware and catch a hint of former tenderness rising in the secret place you knew so well. And just as quickly a sharp comment or flippant remark reminds you why you're not together anymore. Chairs scrape the tiled floor, the bill is paid, and a quick embrace is exchanged.

"Nice to see you." And that's that for another year.

It's an awkward path to walk in the wake of broken relationships, but for the sake of the children it's an important one to stay close to. Over time there's a measure of mellowing, forgiveness and acceptance, with perhaps a greater wisdom and insight that surfaces as time and God heals.

We're on that journey now. It seems to be getting easier as we share graduations and other important occasions around the daughters we both cherish and love.

Jericho Road

He turned the desert into pools of water and the parched ground into flowing springs;
there he brought the hungry to live, and they founded a city where they could settle.
Psalm 107:35-36

They say that seeing is believing.

But believing is also seeing. And I was slowly learning to see in a new paradigm.

Since my superman revelation I was beginning to live from the inside out; making a concerted effort to declare truths I knew to be God's promises. Before, my natural disposition had been to allow my circumstances to dictate how I felt and whether God even cared. Now I was choosing to believe that God is faithful, trustworthy and good – powerful, and more than willing to lead me into restoration. He was a much more reliable source of truth regarding my identity and purpose.

I know this might sound crazy and a little unbelievable in a world and culture so invested in materialism and intellectual understanding. It's about growing in sensitivity to one's spirit. If you'll bear with me I'll try to describe what that signified in my journey. The words in the Bible came to life and provided a foundation and context for my encountering and experiencing God's love that continues to heal my broken identity. It was a world of paradox.

Living subject to fear and unbelief meant playing it safe and making sure I found a job that would pay well to assure a secure financial present and future. My self-reliance caused me to worry and fret over how things would work out instead of entrusting it all to an unseen God revealed in the person of Jesus. Anger and fear held me ransom for so long it intrigued me to actually experience their intensity subsiding as hopeful anticipation and faith grew stronger.

"Keep walking into freedom and trust me," I'd repeat over and over in my head, hearing its echo rise up from the Psalms I read every day.

The whisper of assurance 'looped' in my ear: "Everything I have is yours." Sometimes the Father of the Prodigal Son would catch me in the grace of the homecoming embrace. Other days I was the older brother fighting with him to quell my anger. But with greater frequency now I was hearing the music of forgiveness and love playing, and feeling it's rhythm in my heart. I was responding to the invitation to make myself at home in the same banqueting hall where those brothers were invited to dine (and live) with their father. It was a vibrant community of music, dance, provision, joy, celebration, safety, and unspoken confidence in the resources and presence of the father (a description of a church community – on earth as in heaven). If the story is unfamiliar you can find it in the Bible or Google Luke 15:11-32.

I was learning the depth of a father's love that was unconditional and delighted in me. It was filling the void. Tenderly healing the broken longing and aching disappointment I'd felt when driving away from my earthly father for the last time with an empty wave and 'good luck' as our parting words.

"Why don't you live out of this place with me?" I heard. It was such a different mindset to what I'd grown up with or been accustomed to. God - a loving and generous father - with resources, kindness, power, and passion for me to be with him, and him to be with me. He hadn't disqualified me after all, despite my rage and tantrums, my betrayals and my poor choices. He wasn't even disillusioned with me; just thrilled to be reconciled; as I would be with any of my daughters. My heart hadn't burned within me to this extent for a long time.

This paradigm shift had nothing to do with wishful thinking, not being in touch with reality, or abdicating responsibility. It had everything to do with learning the meaning of faith and responding to the revelation of God revealed through Jesus. It was not religion but relationship initiated by a very good God who is not made in my image and whose ways and thoughts don't come close to what I intuitively grasp or understand by myself.

I began building a website for a new Jericho Road Church even though it did not exist. I had no one to work with, and no members. I figured it wouldn't do any harm to describe a vision and see if anyone was interested in sharing a new adventure. The name had come to mind shortly after the first Graham Cooke conference I'd attended.

Jericho Road was where the man in Jesus' story (about a Good Samaritan) was beaten up and left bleeding, on the busy route between Jerusalem and Jericho. The preoccupied religious leaders passed by not wanting to be inconvenienced or interrupted. Eventually it was a Samaritan, one who was despised himself, who stopped and cared for the wounded victim. Jericho Road symbolized a place that would care for the broken, emphasizing healing for the journey rather than religious orders and rules.

When the website draft was complete I planned to host a pilot group in my home in September with David, one of the people who'd kept in touch over the years from Port Alberni. But the timing wasn't right and we agreed to disband and revisit the idea in a few years.

At the same time a handful of people visited me from Port Alberni expressing anxiety and deep concern about the direction of our former church. I'd been totally disinterested in what was happening there since my departure, both because of my lingering anger and the fact that I could not imagine returning to the role of a pastor ever again. Over the years I attended at Easter and Christmas with my daughters, and was personally alarmed at what I observed from a distance; but then who was I to speak?

Egos and personal ministries were enmeshed in codependent relationships. A culture of Christian spiritual 'speakeasy' had evolved where 'anointing', 'God told me', and 'we need to pray' provided the respectable smokescreens for the fulfilling of more personal agendas. The problem was that there was no 'court of appeal' or real accountability, and therein lies the danger for all of us in any position of spiritual leadership. How ironic that years earlier we'd left a crumbling institutional church and now I was entering an equally dysfunctional 'independent' church.

It was an awkward situation and politically incorrect (an understatement) for me to become involved. Yet I was familiar with the history, knew many of the people in leadership, and was available. I didn't consider for a minute that anything long term would result from this consultation, other than my offering temporary assistance through an unfortunate leadership struggle.

Some who approached me had been members of the church for 30 or 40 years, others for 15 or 20 years. All felt stifled, hopeless, and trapped; yet they still seemed to trust me and value my opinion even though they'd endured the pain and turmoil of my 'fall and betrayal' ten years previously. Back then after my demise I was followed by another pastor whom the church reluctantly asked to leave; a decision that incurred a hefty financial settlement. The present pastor had been with them about six years. They were tired and lacked the resolve or energy to take on yet another leadership challenge. This was not a difficult or demanding community, therefore when the core group began to speak out I knew all was not well.

I offered to interview those in leadership and suggested that perhaps a transition team be formed to bridge the gap as we discerned the road ahead. And so it was that a broken healing man was reintroduced to a broken healing church by a God who never gives up on anyone.

Integrity is hugely important to me and over these months God began to give me a framework for comprehending in part this battle I/we were embroiled in. I was reminded of the words I'd received in my spirit months earlier, "You can be a church that breaks bread in Egypt or you can be a church that breaks bread in the Promised Land; both embrace Christianity but they are very different." I'll explain with broad brush strokes and generalizations.

The Egyptian Church focusses on the Cross, human sinfulness, authority, control, slavery, and freedom through death into heaven. The emphasis is on the negative fallen nature of humanity. God is to be revered and obeyed, the Bible is the only way he speaks, and Christian leadership is entrusted to Priests and Pastors 'who know what's best for you'.

The Church in the Promised Land on the other hand celebrates the resurrection won through the Cross. The focus is on freedom, inheritance, God's Kingdom experienced on earth as in heaven (power to heal, supernatural signs and wonders, extraordinary love and forgiveness) and discovering our true identity as sons and daughters. God is kind, joyful, and vibrant – not at all into control or painting by numbers. He is highly relational and it is His presence and love that draw people into transformation rather than religious conformity and rules.

The Egyptian Church functions through hierarchy and top-heavy authoritarian leadership, programs, conformity, knowing the Bible intellectually, and striving to make a good impression. Society is impacted through political reform, Christian leaders, policies aligned with the Bible, and understanding the distinction between secular and sacred. Egypt lives from the outside in - under the dictum of "Seeing is believing" – faith is in 'self' and originates with human effort, the tangible and intellectual (God helps those who help themselves and science is the final authority).

The Promised Land Church invites everyone to be involved and adopts team leadership. It is highly relational, believing that all life flows from God the Father's love igniting human hearts with a renewed sense of identity, passion and purpose. The Bible is to be read in order to experience God's supernatural presence released on earth through the person of the Holy Spirit. Those occupying the Promised Land approach life from the inside out – "Believing is seeing," – faith is rooted in God's faithfulness, trusting in His promises and leading (God helps those who are in relationship with Him).

Life is lived by faith; often messy and unpredictable but never boring. Society will be impacted through individual and personal encounters with God's love and power just as in the time of Jesus. There is an expectation that God will use anyone who is available and willing and that through ordinary people extraordinary works of healing and breakthrough will be naturally supernatural. There is no distinction between secular and sacred – everything belongs to God.

This emerging metaphor offered me a greater perspective to understand what had happened to me and why so many get stuck in 'church'. It was the larger canvas that made increasing sense as I journeyed out of my personal despair and slavery. It opened up a spiritual paradigm shift revealing the complex overlap between good and evil, the epidemic we call religion, and the revelation and rescue mission of Jesus. It wasn't competing with science (human wisdom arising from an extremely restricted world view/paradigm). Instead it complemented Science by addressing an entirely different question.

Science focusses on exploring and explaining the physical universe and how history has unfolded. Spiritual history is equally fascinating and informative and tackles the 'why' behind the universe and our purpose in it.

The metaphor provided the backdrop for my journey from slavery to freedom giving substance to my faith while still leaving plenty of room for mystery. It's a lifelong adventure – from a grasshopper to a giant mindset, the transformation from slave to a child with an inheritance. It's about being released from an impoverished disempowered slave mentality into becoming a son and daughter of a God revealed as Father who declares, "All I have is yours." It's about rediscovering true identity, "You are my Son/daughter, whom I love and in whom I am well pleased."

It was this rediscovery of my identity (the superman emblem) that broke the logjam and began the journey of restoration. Life flows from a spiritual center within, not external circumstances. If we neglect the reality of our spirits the only resource left is medication – which tackles the chemical and physiological symptoms manifest in our minds and bodies. Of course there is an appropriate place for medication.... But if the spirit is ignored those same medications can act like a manhole cover trapping inside what could be released by God's spirit. And when I'd neglected my spirit I experienced that cover slamming down and darkness descending.

Utilizing a rented community hall and then a school gym Jericho Road began its new life (while a small group opted to remain with the pastor and a building – sharing the details serves no constructive purpose here). It was only the deep friendships, shared commitment and valuing community that enabled us to stay together. As we were reconciled we facilitated discussions to review our respective journeys, angers, disappointments, and concerns for the future. We owned our failures, repented and asked forgiveness where we'd hurt one another, and acknowledged how we might have done things differently. We knew that God's hand was upon us precisely because the situation was so unexpected and our regrouping so bizarre.

My office was a laptop and various coffee shops where I met with people and began the long road of reconstruction and healing. I travelled with others to attend a variety of conferences that would plug us in to what God was doing elsewhere and enable us to find personal and corporate healing and refreshing.

From such rubble and disillusionment Jericho Road was birthed with a determined will and a vision to learn from the past and take hold of the future we trusted God to unveil. But like many God-created deliveries it was messy at times.

The return to ministry in Port Alberni felt like personal suicide as there remained countless skeletons and attitudes (normal in small towns where people know each other, or 'know of'). Many were thrilled to see me while others couldn't come to terms with my being allowed back into the leadership of a church. Furthermore as all of this was unfolding Catherine and I were continuing to see each other.

I sat down with the leadership team of the fledgling Jericho Road and shared my journey again and the situation with Catherine. It would have been predictable, normal, and perhaps wise for them to have backed off. Instead they poured out grace and we agreed to walk together whatever the future held. Nothing was hidden.

Grace was all I had – a gift from the heart of Jesus incarnated through a long-suffering community, totally unmerited - and it saved my life. It's impossible to appreciate God's grace if we have no comprehension of our need – or our state of 'disgrace' without him.

I believe that the Christian church should be a warm and inviting family; where struggling people - even in compromising situations experience unconditional love, acceptance and the opportunity to grow into a better version of themselves. It has nothing to do with tolerating 'sin' and everything to do with loving the 'sinner' deeply enough to facilitate and nurture transformation.

If such grace is denied and Christian masks are preferred then the darker side of our journeys into wholeness merely retreats to fester below the surface. That's the hypocrisy so many outside the church despise.

I'm delighted when people trust me enough to share their struggles. It means God's at work; with exposure to the light healing begins and real freedom breaks out. Everyone on earth is a work in progress.

Becoming a Christian believer merely means that we're now in touch with the One who will continue to work in us and through us to facilitate that very process. Communities formed around Jesus should be the safest most genuine and hope-filled places on earth.

God's love patiently and gently tugged me deeper into trusting him and healing the past. Catherine was also hurting and unresolved. Despite being welcomed and cared for by those who'd known her for years, the prospect of returning to Port Alberni proved too daunting. She attended some events and we were even engaged for a few months while I continued to believe that everything would work out.

I wasn't trying to rebel against God at all, and had already laid everything down before him, including the relationship with Catherine. As time went by some of those close to me began to suggest that it may be time to let go. On the one hand I didn't know how, and on the other I was terrified of messing up this new restoration into ministry or betraying those who had called me again.

Our inability to find mutual peace proved there was indeed too much baggage between Catherine and me and by year's end the relationship finally died. I had to accept that God's hand was over all things including this very painful and vulnerable reality. The person I thought I'd be marrying shut the door and this long tortuous chapter finally ended. I had vowed that I'd never return to ministry alone but also that I'd hold nothing back from him. This time, even in the turmoil I continued to hear God's voice persistently whispering, "Trust me, and keep walking."

Almost every day I return to the story of the Prodigal Son. I lean into the embrace of the passionate loving father who welcomed him/me home with the smells and sounds of a banqueting hall and the whisper, "All I have is yours." I remember how faithfully God drew me out of loneliness and despair and brought me back to the position from where I'd fallen.

This was the last place on earth I ever imagined I'd be; in the same church, the same community, and restored into ministry. And it was only the beginning.

Back To Africa

Where can I go from your Spirit?
Where can I flee from you presence?
If I go up to the heavens, you are there; if I make my bed in the depths, you are there.
If I rise on the wings of the dawn, if I settle on the far side of the sea, even there your hand will guide me, your right hand will hold me fast.
Psalm 139:7-10

Six months later I was on my way to Uganda to conduct a three day teaching seminar and visit an orphanage. I never thought I'd have anything to say nor a heart soft enough to care about others. This was the continent of my birth where I'd first heard the call to know God and follow Jesus

A young Ugandan boy, maybe five years old, chatted excitedly in an English accent with his father and younger sibling. Mimicking the flight path of the airplane his outstretched arm 'whooshed' across the seats. He smiled, bright ivory teeth against his ebony skin, radiating life and secure joy in the presence of his father. I offered my window seat and he was thrilled to watch the lights of London as our aircraft lifted from Heathrow into the darkness of the night sky.

By dawn, we landed; the rain draped grey translucent veils across rich green foliage, the tires skidding then gripping the runway at Entebbe airport in Uganda.

Twenty hours earlier I'd been munching a raisin bran muffin in Vancouver International, a massive complex that could've housed twenty Entebbe airports – statues, waterfalls, food courts, walls of windows, winding avenues of duty free shops, free Wi-Fi and people coming and going everywhere.

I'd settled into one of the seating areas and mused about my trip to follow.

What lay ahead? What would Africa be like? I hadn't set foot on the continent for many years. I was visiting a church in Kampala whose pastor had spoken at Jericho Road the previous year just as we were getting up and running. Because I'd grown up in Africa we enjoyed an immediate affinity and he invited me to come over to Kampala whenever possible. His large church was linked with the university and I was scheduled to conduct teaching sessions during the first week. How would students from Kenya, Tanzania, and Uganda respond? What did I have to offer them?

Then a trip to the northwest was planned for a rural pastors' conference in Nebbi, a remote village across the Nile. If I allowed myself to think about it, I'd be intimidated. Would I be seen as yet another arrogant European parachuting in to rescue the "poor heathen natives?" I knew they faced formidable challenges merely eking out a living and providing food for their families.

The end of my journey into East Africa would be seven days in the slums of Mbarara *(Um-ba-ra-ra)* with a project we supported to help street kids. About 20 boys lived in a compound where they received food and clothing and a sense of home and community while attending school. Pat was a retired teacher who'd been a member of our church in Port Alberni for many years. She began working among street children eight years earlier and I was visiting to see the Jericho Road Children's Project first hand and learn how we might offer support. As she and Micah were working in the same region it was a great opportunity to visit both of them.

Micah, the pastor of the University Community Fellowship welcomed me at the airport. We drove to Makarere University campus where his church gathered in a large green and white striped tent situated in the midst of student residence buildings. At least five hundred students gathered there every Sunday. During the three evening meetings many showed up with enthusiasm and a hunger to experience more of God. It felt good to be back on African soil again.

Every step taken was an affirmation from God that he was restoring me and validating his call on my life. All the broken years were being knit together for me to share with others and declare through my imperfections how kind and gracious he is. If he could redeem my life surely anyone can anticipate the possibility of change. And if sharing the pain of my poor choices and consequences helped someone else find hope that would be amazing.

A few years earlier I would never have dreamed I would be enthusiastically and passionately declaring these truths anywhere, let alone on my home continent of Africa. I marveled at what I was saying probably more than anyone else.

Early Friday morning Micah and I headed out to Nebbi. We bumped our way north along roads unlike anything I'd ever witnessed. Traffic was heavy with trucks, cars, and overladen buses slowing to a crawl, accelerating, and weaving through a moonscape of potholes. Further north we encountered massive vehicles laden with goods from the Sudan careening toward us forcing us onto the muddy shoulder to avoid a possible collision.

"Much of this area has been closed for years," Micah explained as we drove through the Gulu region, "because of the war between the Ugandan People's Defense Force and the Lord's Resistance Army." We passed large camps of displaced people sprawled along the roadside. Blackened shelters of plastic and branches constructed to house families fleeing unthinkable atrocities. Vendors lined the highway hawking meager supplies of fruit, vegetables, and roasted goat meat on sticks.

Along the lush banks of the Nile we spotted a herd of elephants in the distance. A few fishermen in wooden dugouts cracked the mirror surface as we crossed the bridge to stop for a brief visit with Micah's relatives. We sat under a large spreading tree and drank tea before navigating a winding gravel road into the hills to the small conference center.

The center and nearby village had no electricity. Morning and evening children wound their way up and down the hills with buckets of water precariously balanced on their heads. Woman walked miles, heavy loads of grey bundled sticks rhythmically rocking above their headscarves as they chatted together on their way home.

Late at night I sat outside my room under the stars on a remote hillside listening to sounds of Africa; barking dogs, clanging pots, children crying, and long intermittent silences. "It must have been the same a hundred years ago." Africa was seeping back into my soul and

I cherished the 'awakening'. I'd fled this continent in fear of political unrest, incessant violence, and concern for my unborn children's future. I wondered whether in the peace of Canada I'd fallen prey perhaps to comfort and compromise. I couldn't put my finger on it amidst the chorus of night beetles and the cool night air but it was another homecoming and new beginning of sorts.

Just as the journey to England had helped me rediscover the purpose and meaning for my life this African visit touched a part of my spirit and heritage that only God could have understood and helped me reclaim. Maybe it was hope rising, or grace settling within, or even love and humility growing inside the lost little boy at last finding his way in the world.

It was those things for sure, but eventually the key dawned on me like a fiery African sunrise. This time in Africa it felt as if God was placing his stamp of approval on my return to ministry and leadership. Confidence regarding that renewed call released an authority and commission that transcended any denomination or church. When God the father met me as the prodigal son returning home he embraced me in his arms with total acceptance and joy.

However, later, as I ventured back to denominational affiliation I was not greeted with the same quality of unrestrained welcome. It was 'welcome into the office' rather than into our arms. The embrace may follow the test of worthiness.

Far too many people experience 'the desk on the road' on their way to church. Tests have to be passed before there's freedom to proceed. It's meant to be the other way around. There should be a massive bear hug embrace of unconditional acceptance first… with transformation and change to follow within the context of community. Being embraced and validated by the father sets captives and wayward sons and daughters free, and that's how I felt.

The next morning outside their crude house of mud and sticks a man and his son hammered rocks into small stones that would eventually be used for building concrete mix. I watched twenty men crowd into a small room where a donated library from the United States filled the shelves. I looked at some of the titles and wondered who would ever read them as they gleefully squeezed their hulking frames into school desks made for children and fingered the books with awe and enormous pride.

It's the wonder of God that in such a remote place he touches hearts. Men and women intuitively decipher his words germinating within their spirits; responding to a universal search for meaning, significance and hope.

The same hunger was evident over the weekend when we gathered together in the community hall, the most basic building with a concrete floor and a green corrugated roof. More than a hundred leaders in the region including some from the Congo assembled wearing their best clothes, Bibles and notebooks in hand. The women carried themselves with aristocratic poise and dignity in brightly colored long dresses with wide sashes (gomesi). I wondered whether the styles had their origins in the dress of the first European missionaries they encountered perhaps in the 19th century or even earlier.

I was ushered to the stage alongside Micah and a few other pastors who'd be speaking. A young man stood at a battered electric piano powered by a noisy generator accompanied by another two plucking adungus (a unique African stringed instrument)

Nothing compares to African worship. It's impossible not to sing and move to the rhythm. When the musicians led in a song about stepping into the Promised Land the hall erupted with singing, laughter, shouts and whistles. Micah whispered that they were re-enacting the long journey out of slavery to freedom. They sang and danced, hoisting chairs, stools, and even benches over their heads; the jubilant men and women whirling around the room.

I joined in the festivities with a Bible on my head carried along by the music and making up words because I couldn't keep quiet. In this obscure corner of the earth I thanked God I had something to celebrate with a dance of praise that transcended language and cultural barriers.

I danced over the grave of a decade of dark memories when I lost my way in a valley from which I thought I'd never return. I danced over those wasted years of slavery and deception, and I danced in the light of my new-found freedom and restored identity. Joy was rising; and if anyone knows how to pull it out of you it's African Christians. Despite being all too familiar with suffering and poverty joy bubbles to the surface and sets feet a dancin'! The one who came to speak was spoken to.

After the conference we returned to Kampala. The plan was to meet Pat and travel four hours to Mbarara with a pastor who helped her with the orphanage. What I forgot was that invariably "African Time" prevails when setting a schedule. Two hours later than planned, we finally embarked on the road south out of Kampala through the maze of streets and bustling humanity.

We had two extra passengers riding with us in the well-worn car with broken seats, non-existent shock absorbers, and a balding rear tire. Every pothole not successfully avoided produced a thud in my seat and a corresponding bang of my head hitting the roof. Laughter broke out amongst the Ugandan pastors as the "muzungu" (the white person) in the back seat emitted cries and grunts with every bump on the rump.

"Trust in God," they exhorted with friendly laughter.

We stopped on the Equator for photographs and bought freshly caught fish which were tied over the radiator at the front of the car to "keep cool". We pulled in at another town for gas and slowed down when roadside vendors tempted our driver with fried bananas, fruits, and goat meat skewered on sticks.

It was nearly ten o'clock in the evening when we rattled into Mbarara and carefully idled down one more eroded street to the compound where the boys lived. I was weary and frustrated that a four-hour trip had been hammered into seven and a half hours of extreme endurance.

The boys were delighted to greet us, chattering and bouncing around – they hadn't seen their beloved Pat for six months. I was proudly shown to my room – a dirty-walled concrete square with a hideous pink mosquito net draped above a single bed. A square of linoleum covered one third of the concrete floor. A noisy freezer that had seen better days sounded as if it was chewing ice in one corner, and a small bookshelf with a few plates behind a curtain completed the furnishings. A can of 'Raid' tastefully placed beside the bed hinted at the presence of a few nocturnal visitors.

A well-used plastered tool shed had been emptied out and painted, proudly presented to me as my private washing area complete with a blue plastic basin and a new sponge. The toilet was a 2ft x 4ft concrete room with a square opening in the floor. Three of them side by side, two for the boys and one for me.

"From Vancouver to this…" I muttered behind a polite smile. I was tired and wanted to retreat into my own company. But I was not alone and as I reflected on the uncomfortable journey, and the threadbare facilities God whispered to my spirit, "What did you expect? This is hope, love, food and a home these boys have never known. Besides, what do you think I did for you?"

By the end of the week I felt as if I'd been there for months. On the second evening the goat that greeted me with wide-eyed curiosity on my arrival was roasting on a coal fire, her head lying in the grass. The night before I left the boys dressed up in various costumes, danced, and played drums in the courtyard outside.

As we crowded into a small room singing songs and talking about God, the boys' laughter quickly changed when we considered the love of the father. A deep silence settled over the room. They had so little – Pat had found most of them on the streets without a home, their parents dead from aids, running from horrible situations. Many recounted how they used to drink at night because it helped them sleep; some of them were younger than twelve years old.

My childhood was nothing compared to their situations. I wanted to stay and help build this humble community, be a father to them. A young boy knocked on my door and shyly asked me to pray for him, he had a kidney disease and a deformed leg. We chatted for a while before I laid my hands on him and prayed for God's love and power to touch him.

"Let your Kingdom come Lord, on earth as in heaven." I later learned his kidneys had been healed.

Early the next morning I slipped out on a "border-border" – a motorcycle taxi - to get to the bus station while it was still dark and the boys were asleep. The bus was crowded and I prayed for a safe trip to Kampala. Considering the last 12 years of barrenness, I realized the potholes were nothing compared to the journey I'd already completed.

The last time I left Africa my father was dying and I was heading into the worst decade of my life. I believed then that God had abandoned me as an orphan. Now, all things were being made new. The superman emblem was emblazoned on my chest. I had a new identity. *All the Father has is mine*, I thought. *I am a much loved son with a future, walking into an inheritance beyond what I could ever ask for or imagine.*

I knew in my spirit that this revelation, revolution, and rebirth was a miracle.

The Promised Land

For you, Lord, have delivered me from death, my eyes from tears, my feet from stumbling, that I may walk before the Lord in the land of the living.
Psalm 116:8-9

Sometimes God moves ever so slowly and on other occasions acceleration is underway and hold on to your hat!

The most exhilarating breakthrough for me was that I was no longer wandering alone. I was experiencing the love of God my Father on the inside – blossoming into a confidence and hope that touched every aspect of my life. And I was being reintegrated into a church; a community where relationships were strong and ran deep. These people were actually my family.

I was also learning that like any caring father nothing we regard as important is dismissed or trivialized by God. As seeds of negativity often sprout from the most innocent of origins and explode into giant beanstalks when unchecked, so too the positive and constructive usually germinates within the everyday events of our lives. Such was the case with Sheryl.

Fifteen years earlier I had met her briefly in a counselling situation and then bumped into her while watching my daughter play soccer one Saturday morning. At that stage I was not in a great space. "You were in a foul mood," she later told me. "Were you shocked?" I asked. "Not really, I was actually glad to meet someone who expressed something of what I was feeling."

Five years later as Jericho Road was starting out Sheryl began attending a midweek group that I was leading. A friend of hers wondered whether I could help her find healing from depression and we began to meet (the three of us) for counselling. I do this a lot so it was not out of the ordinary. What was extraordinary was the day I drove into town and asked the Lord what would be helpful when I met with Sheryl and her friend. Out of nowhere I was given the idea to buy her a puzzle. "Buy a puzzle and place the pieces in a plastic bag and leave the box with the picture in your car."

I was intrigued and found some puzzles at a local store. Most of them were not appropriate until tucked in the back of a shelf I found a relatively simple puzzle – a picture with a cozy house overlooking a safe harbor. On a hill behind it was a lighthouse beaming light and I wondered whether it had a message of encouragement as well. I've never in twenty five years had such a nudge.

That afternoon as we began our conversation I handed Sheryl the puzzle in the plastic bag and she was rather mystified. "I hate doing puzzles," she said, "I never know where pieces go and they don't get finished." "Why don't you go to my car and fetch the box," I suggested. When she returned she obviously could now see the picture. Would it be easier to do the puzzle with or without the picture in front of you?" I asked. "Much easier with the picture of course," she replied.

"I think God wants you to have this puzzle because he's making you a promise. As you work on the puzzle with Jesus by your side he will begin to fix the broken parts of your life. I believe this picture is what he wants to be for you, a place of safety and a shelter from storms."

Sheryl told me later she took it home and didn't touch it for a while. When she finally began tears streamed down her face. The pieces came together so easily and she knew the presence of the Lord was in her room as she worked on it.

Months later during one of my solitary journeys home I pondered the fact that I was not the only one who was lonely. I knew that Sheryl was sitting around doing nothing; maybe we could hang out together and be friends. Unbeknown to me something was stirring in her as well.

Sheryl endured her own challenges; seven years alone raising two children and working with special needs children in schools. She too unwittingly lost her way in Egypt where depression and loneliness overwhelmed her.

That is - until Jesus showed up quite unexpectedly in her living room one ordinary Wednesday afternoon and gently posed a question that took her breath away. I asked her to share her story:

I lived in solitude for seven years, not wanting anyone in my space, not trusting men, not wanting anything to do with men. I was alone and loving it, proud to be someone who needed no one around me. I worked hard at believing that and I did it well - or so I thought.

Saying 'yes' to Jesus brings unexpected events. What happened next is amazing to me - an absolute miracle.

I was sitting on my chair in my small rented house. I'd taken pride in decorating it and making it a 'home' for the children and me. It was full of knick-knacks, an eclectic collection of Dutch 'stuff' from my parents and other antiques (I love scrounging for treasures in antique stores and garage sales). As usual I was 'home alone' after school – depressed, crying, angry, and enjoying my pity party. Suddenly my misery was interrupted by someone speaking, "What do you want?" Distracted from my 'party' for a moment I wondered what that could mean? Again I heard the gentle question, "What do you want?" Then I knew Jesus was talking to me - he was sitting on the couch across from me – I sensed his presence.

I knew straight away what he was asking me; and I intuitively knew that he knew that I knew – which was scary. God knows everything and it was not a time for avoidance and bullshit – I knew that too! Jesus was asking me what I wanted. How could I tell him that what I wanted was what I had been denying all along? So with attitude (behind every depressed person with a demure demeanor there's a will of steel) I replied, "Fine, I'll tell you what I want. I want to be loved, I want to be held, I want to be touched, and I want someone to share my dreams and thoughts with. I want to be heard, I want to be understood, I want to be accepted, I want to cuddle on the couch, I want... someone to love my toes... I want... I want...

Tears streamed down my face as I told Jesus my most intimate desires that I'd not confessed to myself for years and years. I sobbed, uncontrollable weeping, angry that he was making me say these things. They were lies inside my head that I sincerely believed but despite myself the truth was coming out of my mouth. My mind screamed in the background, "No, you don't want these things; you promised yourself you'd never ever want again – you fool!"

I ended with a flourish... "There, are you happy? I told you what I want, now you deal with it!" and I stormed out of the room. Can you imagine leaving God sitting on your couch? I did.

The next morning when I woke up I was excited in a strange way; I had an anxious/anticipation feeling, something was different. Two days after I told God what I wanted for the first time in seven years I was asked out on a date. Shocked, shy, and knowing 'this was it' I said 'yes'.

Three days after Sheryl somewhat reluctantly revealed her heart to God on the couch we went to a movie recommended by my daughter – *The Bucket List*. Michelle said that when she saw the story of two men drawing up lists and then stepping out to fulfill their dreams she thought of me. I was curious to see what she meant.

Afterwards Sheryl and I sat with our feet up by the fire at a local pub and chatted many hours away. She hadn't been on a real date for seven years and our easy conversation had been something I'd missed for a long time. An unexpected peace surrounded us that night. We discussed our histories openly and without tension. She had been quite friendly with Karin after we'd divorced and I was out of town. "I don't blame her for not wanting to take you back," Sheryl asserted. "Try that with me and I'll have the U-Haul truck in the driveway and be gone."

"You're deceptively strong beneath that mellow exterior," I said. I would grow to learn that Sheryl is also extremely discerning and reads me like a book, unafraid to challenge me. "Don't turn what I've just said back on me now….."

Having both weathered turbulent waters we were quite content to take a day at a time and see what happened. I'd been on such a merry-go-around for years spending time with Sheryl was like finding a safe harbor (maybe that puzzle picture had been for me as well?). Still, for many months I was wary, wondering when something would go wrong. Throughout our initial friendship she was amazingly accepting and unthreatened; our weekends and evenings together increased with the easy enjoyment of one another's company.

I felt seen and understood by her and she told me she felt the same. I knew I'd claimed to have experienced that before but this time it was different; less tenuous, a more natural, secure, and legitimate foundation. I admired her resilience in tough times to provide for her son and daughter and the close relationship she enjoyed with both of them. She worked two jobs, often for long hours to make ends meet, and demonstrated a deep empathy and compassion for the special needs people others passed by.

Since circumstances over the past few years had been so jarring and wrenching, I wasn't expecting to be in another relationship so soon. Of course I was extremely aware of my responsibility as a pastor and the grace extended to me and I was absolutely committed to honoring that trust. So it surprised me to find such easy comfort with Sheryl.

The most amazing gift for me was her acceptance of who I was without any pressure or demands. She wasn't afraid to acknowledge our mutual baggage and never responded with jealousy or a sense of being threatened. At the same time she was as astonished as I was that God would open up a relationship for us after all we'd been through.

Five months passed, including my trip to Uganda, and there was time to reflect on where we were going. It's strange how sometimes you just know that you know, and we realized that our relationship could be moving fast toward a more permanent commitment. I requested and received positive affirmation from the leadership of Jericho Road regarding our blossoming friendship. I was awed by God's gentle provision and the affirmation he gave us through our friends and community.

I was extremely humbled by their faith and willingness to walk with me again and I wanted to honor their grace by submitting my relationship to them. If they'd presented concerns or red flags I would have pulled back. In fact they were thrilled; they'd accompanied Sheryl on her journey for many years and responded with two thumbs up.

It was a joy to be in a community that could help discern big decisions with me, rather than what I'd known previously, relying solely on my perspective. I was so grateful that everything was entirely voluntary and I never felt pressured to share anything. It was not about being controlled and more about sharing my life and receiving help and insight so that I didn't just rush ahead into more turmoil. That's the wonderful gift of community when it works well.

It was a Sunday evening in July. Sheryl sat in the arm chair across the room from me when I made my move.

"What are you doing on Friday?" I asked, trying to be casual and cool.

"I'm not sure," she responded hesitatingly.

"It's your birthday isn't it?" I asked.

"Yes."

"How about we get married then as well?" I said with a smile.

"What? In four days? Are you serious?"

"Sure, we'll have a small ceremony with only the children present – at Dave and Megan's house. That way no-one will be offended about not being invited and we can have a reception for everyone later."

"Oh my goodness," Sheryl laughed. "I'll have to buy a dress!"

Friday came and the sun was shining. Sheryl looked lovely in a yellow dress, and we exchanged vows in front of our children giving thanks to God for his healing grace and goodness. We gave God all our old baggage; looked into each other's eyes and promised to love and cherish one another "until death do us part."

After a short honeymoon aboard a friend's boat on the West Coast I continued to work with Jericho Road in Port Alberni and Sheryl resumed her patient empathic support of a severely handicapped boy. She moved into my rustic house, filled it with some of her furniture and hundreds of 'nick-knacks', and at long last transformed it into our home.

Perhaps that puzzle was meant for both of us, where the lighthouse was God protecting us from future danger and the cabin by a secluded bay offered a home of safety and refuge. Having attempted to snatch at solutions with disastrous results my peace and contentment were at last coming from within. I no longer felt abandoned nor betrayed by God. I could live with a sense of mystery and the yearning for a mother quietened within my soul.

Every now and again I see a picture or a character in a movie that reminds me of my mother and I feel an appropriate ache. But it no longer leads me to a negative place and I can move on. We all walk with limps and scars. I'm becoming used to Sheryl's sensitivity, acceptance, and empathic ways and she's helping me soften in areas where my protective walls have stood firm for so long I thought they were 'just the way I am'. Those defenses are gradually melting and of course is an ongoing work in process. Sheryl hates me saying that because it sounds like an excuse; but it's not meant to be.

Sheryl and I have been married for over six years now. We've enjoyed holidays we never thought we'd have. One year we visited the east coast of Australia to visit my brother and his family in Brisbane.

Another Christmas a friend generously invited us to Cape Town to celebrate our sixtieth birthdays and paid for the airfares. We spent three glorious weeks in their summer exploring my childhood haunts and reconnecting with old friends. Sheryl didn't want to leave. "Take me back to the beaches of Cape Town," she pleads whenever it's cold and raining here on Vancouver Island – which is often.

Meanwhile the Jericho Road community that welcomed me back into their hearts so graciously has also experienced wonderful healing and restoration. We bought a small building that had been used as an Orthodox Church and held weekly activities there while continuing to rent a school gym for Sundays. Every week we set up equipment and chairs while God slowly restored within us a new level of trust and hope for the future.

My office in a local coffee shop continued for over three years. Until the few remaining members of the other portion of the church (who kept the building) approached us after their pastor departed. They were convicted that the Lord was telling them to give the church building back to us and to seek reconciliation. It was a joy and pleasure to respond with an exuberant, "Yes, of course!"

Within a few weeks we held a service of reconciliation where we publicly repented together for the part we each played in our flawed and fractured history. That included an honest appraisal of what had happened and taking responsibility for our decisions and actions; there were no hands innocent of blood in this scenario. We asked God to forgive us and to restore us into one fellowship. It was a moving and poignant gathering that marked a new beginning. It was quite unbelievable. I marveled in my heart and spirit at how God works to redeem and restore those of us who so easily become broken, lost, and disconnected.

The building we returned to was initially a large middle school of 65,000 square feet. I remember the first Tuesday alone in the upstairs area in this vast complex. I sat at a table and wondered what on earth we had taken on. All the poison and negativity of the last years filled the atmosphere as the fear and sense of heaviness rose up again. I felt the pain of friends who were angry and betrayed and how dreams had been shattered spreading discontent in every direction.

The next Thursday we gathered the church community together and walked around every inch of the property praying and declaring God's grace and Kingdom to be present. From that time I sensed the Lord directing us to not be afraid, to step into this Promised Land again and take it – remembering that, "Believing is seeing." I already had a testimony of God's faithfulness to the promise he gave me, "You work on the house and I'll work on you."

The reclaiming of the building was a significant metaphor that stretched us to the limit. We established a leadership team and began to paint walls and slowly redecorate the facility as a tangible sign of our faith to establish what appeared at times impossible.

Five years later we're still there and the church is growing. The inside is unrecognizable thanks to the hard work and generosity of many who have contributed to the transformation. All our available space is now shared and rented.

An equally important development over the past few years has been an emerging work with men and women struggling with addictions. On Thursdays a group gathers around a simple meal to support and encourage one another. We're witnessing firsthand how Jesus sets captives free through his love, friendship, and the acceptance of a welcoming community.

I wish I could introduce you to a man who sat in my office sixteen months ago and cried for a relationship he never knew with his father. For the first time in forty years he told me he felt loved and accepted and he gives all honor to Jesus (unfortunately at the time of proofreading this draft he has relapsed, which is a sadly common reality as love causes many to run scared). Or the father of three who discovered the love of Jesus by sensing His presence in the sanctuary and now knows Him as a friend. Or two women who struggled for over twenty years with addictions that led them to the brink of death. It took them through the ravaging and abusive lifestyles of prostitution and multiple sources of substance abuse. While AA was instrumental in their initial recovery it was the Higher Power revealed in the person of Jesus who has loved them into a new life inheriting the Promised Land.

My calendar is booked every week with men and women looking for hope yet powerless to become free on their own. I think they talk to me because I understand brokenness and what it's like to be paralyzed and bleeding at the side of the road. I remember how Jesus came to me and I boast to them of the power of his love that will restore them as they dare to become part of a loving and accepting community.

In the last six months James joined us; thirty years old with a background of foster care, multiple relationships, addiction, violence and jail. Last week we asked God to change his heart of stone to a heart of flesh. He walked across to a table and randomly opened a bible to the promise in Ezekiel 11:19 *"I will give them an undivided heart and put a new spirit in them; I will remove from then their heart of stone and give them a heart of flesh."*

"John, look at this," James said, "What you just prayed for me is in the bible, I've never read this before; I'm so pumped!" That evening he cried for the first time in many years as his heart truly is being changed. "I've never felt so loved and accepted in a community before," he says. I'm moved by God's kindness when he uses the scarred and incomplete men and women we are to touch the lives of those whom he loves with such tenderness and passion.

And who introduced me to James? Jean Francois, a man who has battled with addiction for twenty years. We've been supporting him for many years but particularly in the last two. He's more settled and clear-headed today than as far back as he can remember. He boasts that he would never have been at this level of recovery without the community and others marvel at the progress of someone they'd given up on. He said, "James, you've got to come here, we can help each other." And that's' exactly what's happened.

It's not the brokenness we focus on but the hope for a future that God offers everyone who comes to him. Many have drifted into apathy and are scared of trying or trusting because they're tired of being disappointed; it's better not to feel. On top of that the churches many were associated with had little tolerance for honesty or failure, so they understandably expected the same from me.

I love encouraging them to find out for themselves, "You'll never be rejected here, you may not agree with everything or like all that is said, but that's when we have the opportunity to work things out together."

"It's as if we spend our lives walking backwards into the future," I share. "We're prisoners of our past and tend to define ourselves by what has happened to us. When we meet Jesus he turns us around and invites us to find purpose and identity rooted in who he's made us to be and where we're heading with him. It's who I'm becoming that determines who I am."

Some are scared and sabotage the process. That's ok, when they're ready they'll be back and we'll continue forward because we know the nature of the battle we're engaged in. My life has never been more full and meaningful as I see how God has taken my brokenness and used it to inspire others. I share Paul's testimony that as I boast about my weakness I get to proclaim the goodness and kindness of a God who never stops loving.

Last year in November 2013 I was in South East India where Jericho Road is building what we hope will be a long-term relationship to support an orphanage (Faith India Ministries) for young children. They invited me speak in a village for two nights about the love of Jesus and conduct two days of teaching with two hundred local pastors. Who would have thought?

We're not an isolated church but are affiliated to the Anglican Mission in Canada and the United States; and I'm part of the Canadian Leadership team… imagine!. It's young initiative arising from institutional brokenness with lots to learn but a heart for authenticity, new expressions, and relational community rooted in Jesus.

Even as I write these words I'm in awe of what God has done. I'm sitting at the same desk, looking out of the same window I did when I cried out to God wondering how on earth my journey back into ministry would unfold. When there was $300 in the bank and no logical or rational way forward that I could figure out.

God is indeed good and faithful, and continues to speak, encourage, provide, and lead into adventures beyond my wildest dreams or imagination.

Epilogue

If God can restore my identity there's hope for everyone.

Hearing God is easier than you think…. Listen through your heart.

If you've heard the voice of anger, jealousy, fear, or apathy then you'll know that spiritual voices speak from the inside. Many of us assume God's voice is angry, or will be loud and obvious. It's not like that at all. The first thing to listen for in order to discern good from evil is the tone. The 'voice' will usually manifest as thoughts or nudges that initially sound as if you're talking to yourself.

Evil accuses and attacks our identity with shame magnifying our unworthiness, our failure and our inadequacy. The phrases usually are in the form of accusations such as: "You're pathetic, you'll never succeed, and you're a failure….."

God, on the other hand, always addresses us by name and affirms his love and our identity before mention of anything else. He never accuses and always invites us into relationship where he can give us what is required for the way ahead. As with any relationship, the better we know someone the more clearly we will recognize their voice and distinguish their words from ours.

To identify what God's voice sounds like I encourage you to find an easy-to-read bible (lots of versions Online) and read about Jesus' life and relationships. You'll find accounts in Mark, Luke, Matthew, John….. Mark is the shortest. Read how the early church began in Acts and then start over again. Leave out parts that are hard to understand and focus on how Jesus interacted with ordinary people and you'll find his voice lifting off the page and including you in the conversation. Find other people who are following Jesus and learn from them. Ask questions.

If you want to hear God's voice right now pick a number between 1 - 150. Find the section on Psalms in the Bible and turn to the number you selected. If it speaks to your heart then keep that as a special word from God's heart to yours. If it does not resonate, pick another until the words thrill you. Receive them as his promise for you. God plays games with his kids like any father does. Activities that we think are random he will use. So have fun and expectation.

Engage God with your heart and beware of allowing your head to interrupt all the time… God is unbelievable and is seldom accessed through the rational mind (it's too limited and small to contain him and his ways.) He will speak through thoughts, emotions, circumstances, dreams, music, what you read, movies, friends, and anything else you might imagine.

When I lay on the back benches in Toronto twelve years ago and wandered in the wilderness for eight years, I never expected that my life and ministry could be restored. Everything I'm involved with today I vowed I would not risk or attempt again. I was rejected by many and had given up on myself, but God wasn't done with me yet. I never believed that one day I'd look back and find it hard to imagine what depression was like. I couldn't have written this script or truthfully conceived of such restoration and reconciliation.

As we conclude this journey together, please know that the work of restoration never ends; I'm still very much a work in progress – just ask Sheryl? Neither does our need for one another ever diminish. God has absolutely no favorites, so if there's anything encouraging in these pages that you'd like to claim for yourself just take hold of it and make it your own.

By the way, you also have a Superman emblem emblazoned on your chest; it's part of every human being's DNA placed there by God the Father. He's at your side right now. All you have to do is authentically talk to him without slamming the door and give him permission to ignite your spirit with his love. At least give him a chance to respond – then watch out, because he will. How can a father reject a much loved son or daughter who wants to return home? When you hear him whispering in your ear his words will be filled with delight and affirmation as he calls you by name.

One thing I know for sure. He'll wrap you in the warmest embrace you've ever experienced and say, "You had me at hello." His kiss will bring you to life and release healing in your heart.

That's the reason I've opened my heart to you, I don't want to keep his amazing grace to myself and he has more than enough to share with you too. I look forward to reading your story.

A Prayer

Thank you Father God for the person reading these words right now. I bless them in the name of Jesus and declare the love of the Father's heart to touch them in a manner that will be authentic, real, and personal. I bless your hand upon their lives and the purposes and plans you have for their future. I pray they will be expectant and hope-filled and that you will surround them with friends and community to accelerate their encounter with your healing love and grace.

Thank you that you have no favorites and that you speak over them with great affection, "You are my son/daughter whom I love, and in whom I am well pleased." Wherever there is disappointment, disillusionment, or a loss of hope I ask that you pour out your healing and restoration – more than they could ever imagine. Give them a glimpse of your goodness and an assurance that you will never leave them or forsake them.

And I ask that they will find answers to every question, compassion, validation and healing for every hurt, and a supernatural excitement and assurance for a fulfilling and powerful future. In Jesus' name, Amen

A Short Interview

Question: *Why did you want to share your story, particularly as it involved dredging up a lot of awkward and negative situations?*

John: I've spent much of my life in and around the Christian community and I believe we need to learn how to embrace one another in the process of change. Christianity is not about perfection but rather about encountering the One who loves and restores what is broken. I wonder whether we don't need to listen more to one another's story's before too hastily saying what we think is their answer. I'm not talking about quoting the bible but rather how to share God's words in a manner that brings life rather than condemnation. The only story I can tell is my own, with the prayer that it will provide some measure of encouragement and hope to others who have experienced failure and disappointment along the way.

Question: *Do you think somebody who doesn't believe in God will make sense of your story?*

John: I hope so. I've written with them in mind because I can empathize with disillusionment and cynicism toward Christians and the Church. However I also believe that many people have an inaccurate perception of who God is. It's either, 'anything goes', "the church is irrelevant", or "I don't believe in God". I think people are spiritually hungry and perhaps haven't had the opportunity to explore what that might mean. Imagine if God is real, personal, and much kinder than we ever realized. How cool would that be, and why wouldn't I want to know him and be known by him? My story attempts to highlight his personality and character and demonstrate how a relationship with him is relevant and life changing.

Question: *What about the Church?*

John: That's a big subject. I've attempted to honestly admit that the institutional church is woefully dysfunctional and often a very poor representative of who God is. Nevertheless we are social beings and we gather together around all manner of interests and projects. Growing with God together is no different. In fact it's in community we recognize how much we need his presence, his love, and his healing in our lives. Rather than being shocked by 'issues' we should be thrilled they are rising to the surface so they can be healed. The Church should be the safest place on earth for wounded people to experience acceptance, forgiveness, and hope for a better future.

Question: *What's the greatest lesson you've learned?*

John: That God is good, and he can handle my questioning even when expressed in anger. He never gives up on me and that the supernatural perspective and power he brings to life changes everything. Nothing is impossible for him; never say never, and that encountering his love heals broken hearts and brings freedom to captives.

Question: *What's the key to experiencing God?*

John: Read the stories of Jesus in the Bible – because he is the only spiritual leader who claimed to be God. Be aware that your intellect will never comprehend the mystery of God but an open heart can experience and encounter what the mind cannot process. When I ask God to touch my heart I'll find my thinking changes. And if you get stuck consider what your relationship was like with your earthly father and family and how it may impact your responses. That's why I've shared my background. It's not about blaming but rather learning and understanding in order to grow into a future free of the imperfections and negativity of the past. Never journey alone, supportive relationships accelerate growth. There's so much more I could say but that's a beginning.

Copies of John Cox's CD **'Running Free'** are available from the Jericho Road Church website: jerichoroad-church.com Or download from iTunes

The CD contains some of the songs I wrote as I was coming out of my wilderness – often their truth only settled in my life two years later – but they were seeds God nurtured.

The poetry/prose is available on Kindle: **Into Depression and Beyond** - My *editor, whom I totally respect, told me that it's 'bad poetry'. I responded with a smile that I wasn't trying to write good poetry but rather give expression to the turmoil of depression. Particularly when I felt God had abandoned me as well. In the midst of despair it's hard for others to comprehend the battle that rages within.*

Googling God is an invitation to consider the reality and existence of a personal, loving, and kind God without losing your mind. I'm revising it with the intent to republish by the end of 2014.

Contact: **johncox@jerichoroad-church.com**

About the Author

Born in Cape Town, South Africa, John Cox attended Bishops School, completed his compulsory military service, and earned a BA in psychology from Cape Town University, a certificate of theology from Oxford University's Wycliffe Hall, and a BD from London University. Ordained in the Anglican Church, he served for a few years in Cape Town before immigrating to Vancouver Island, Canada, with his wife to lead St. Alban's Church in Port Alberni as its senior pastor. After twelve years, John's personal life started to unravel—resulting in his resignation from ministry, a divorce, a crisis of faith, and depression. But, by the restorative grace of God, he eventually experienced healing and renewal and returned to the ministry he thought he'd left forever.

John is now married, and he and his wife have four adult children between them. A lifelong learner, he went on to earn an MA in leadership and development from Royal Roads. He is also the author of *Googling God*. John is currently Senior Pastor of Jericho Road Church on Vancouver Island, Canada.

www.ingramcontent.com/pod-product-compliance
Lightning Source LLC
LaVergne TN
LVHW051520070426
835507LV00023B/3210